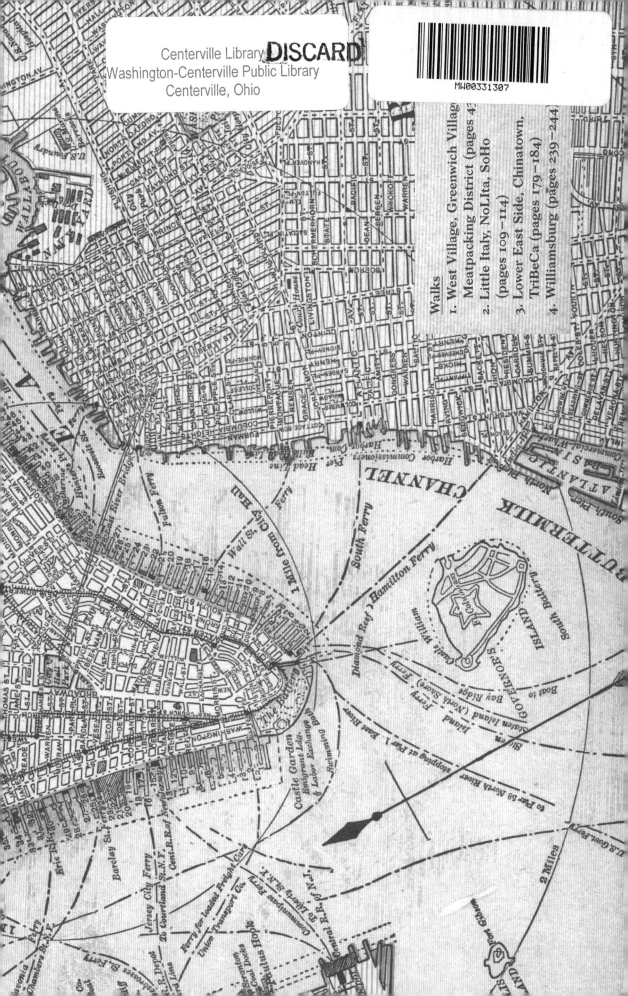

Walks

1. West Village, Greenwich Village, Meatpacking District (pages 4?)
2. Little Italy, NoLIta, SoHo (pages 109–114)
3. Lower East Side, Chinatown, TriBeCa (pages 179–184)
4. Williamsburg (pages 239–244)

SPUNTINO

COMFORT FOOD (NEW YORK STYLE)

RUSSELL NORMAN

Photography by **JENNY ZARINS**

B L O O M S B U R Y
LONDON · OXFORD · NEW YORK · NEW DELHI · SYDNEY

WALK

DON'T WALK

Brunch

Spuntini & Toasts

Pizzette

Salads & Dressings

Sliders

Fish Plates

Meat Plates

Desserts

Drinks

My love affair with New York started many years before I first visited the city, through the cop movies and bad TV shows of my 1970s childhood. From afar the place was mesmerising, and I became increasingly intrigued. I had never thought of a city as a character before, but here was one that seemed vital, visceral, assured, arrogant, cultured, dangerous, sexy and elegant all at once. By the time I finally landed at John F. Kennedy Airport in 1999 I was well on the way to full-blown obsession. On the flight I had felt disproportionately nervous, but not because of the usual flying jitters. I was apprehensive about meeting the long-term object of my long-distance infatuation. In the cab from the airport, as the iconic skyline loomed, all I could hear in my head was Gershwin's 'Rhapsody in Blue', Woody Allen's choice of soundtrack for *Manhattan*. What chance did I have? I was totally smitten.

My first encounter with New York did not disappoint. It is, after all, the ultimate city. It is electric, seemingly generating its own energy, and when you are there, you feel like you are at the centre of the universe. Subsequent visits only served to reinforce my feelings. As I became more familiar with its topographic, gastronomic and cultural landscape, the city revealed itself more fully and filled my heart more completely.

But New York is a metropolis of many layers. Its neighbourhoods and communities differ vastly, depending on where you find yourself, and I quickly discovered my comfort zone. The glitzy society world of the Upper East Side – black-tie benefit bashes and Fifth Avenue shopping trips – was not what I had in mind. I identified with the city of Popeye Doyle in *The French Connection* or Travis Bickle in *Taxi Driver*: gritty and muscular, with more than a modicum of nostalgia. To be honest, I was only really interested in what was happening downtown below 14th Street, where the canyons of tall buildings give way to a cityscape that is more intimate and villagey and where the grid starts to go wonky. Occasionally I would venture across the East River into Williamsburg.

As my tourist's sensibilities evolved, I learnt to see the city as a native might; not looking up in awe at the skyscrapers, bright lights and monuments, but with a horizontal gaze, appraising the streets, the sidewalk, the people, the shopfronts, the doorways, the windows and the businesses behind them. I also started to think about how I might possibly capture something of New York's intangible mojo, bottle it up and bring it across the Atlantic.

The idea for the restaurant first came to me on a research trip with my business partner Richard in 2009. I was amused that the origins of many classic American dishes were, in fact, Italian. Meatballs, pizza, macaroni cheese. I wondered whether a scruffy small-plate joint serving strong cocktails and Italian/American comfort food with a scratchy blues soundtrack was the sort of place people might like in London. The idea became a notebook, the notebook became a business plan, the business plan became a project, and then we just had to find a suitable site. I settled on the name SPUNTINO – the Italian word for 'snack'.

Back in London, we homed in on Soho, bastion of bohemia, carousing and merrymaking, the last neighbourhood in central London where you could buy drugs or sex openly on the street. This may not sound like the ideal location for a restaurant, perhaps, but it appealed to me; just like New York's East Village resonates with 1970s seediness, so too London's Soho thrills and titillates with links to the sleazy 1950s.

We set our hearts on the site of a curry house for sale on Rupert Street, right in the heart of the red-light district. We immediately offered the asking price, but after several weeks of silence, while we assumed that the owner, Mr Jaba, was instructing solicitors, we heard he had changed his mind; the site was not for sale. We were bitterly disappointed and continued our hunt, but no other location had the same feeling of being in the dangerous heart of the city.

A few months later, Mr Jaba had changed his mind again – were we still interested? Without hesitation I said yes and we started the legal process to transfer the lease. Progress was slow but after several months we agreed a date for exchange. In November 2010, we finally completed and could start building work. My plans for the interior involved stripping back the existing plasterwork to see what lay beneath. And what we found was unexpectedly delightful. There were extensive areas of Victorian glazed bricks. An intricate mosaic at ceiling height hinted that the building might once have been a dairy or a fishmonger's. There was a skylight, hidden for decades behind panelling, and an original brick arch beneath four inches of render. Everything else we salvaged from other buildings in various states of demolition, including a Georgian timber floor, an American tin ceiling and several 1950s gooseneck lamps that I bought in a garage flea market on West 25th Street. We hung framed blueprints showing mechanical parts used in the construction of the New York subway that Richard found in a junkyard in Williamsburg.

While our founding head chef Rachel O'Sullivan flew to New York to eat her way around the city, we put the finishing touches to the restaurant – a popcorn machine, a pewter-topped bar, a 1930s cinema EXIT sign, two gumball machines. I asked my five-year-old daughter Martha to write the word 'Spuntino' for me, then faithfully copied it in chalk onto the rusted steel fascia, where it remains (faintly) to this day.

SPUNTINO opened without fanfare on St Patrick's Day, 2011. It is small, with only 27 stools and some standing room. The idea of taking reservations seemed ludicrous in such a tiny space so we didn't. We never even got round to installing a telephone. And it's still that way today.

Brunch

Brunch, as everyone knows, is a classic portmanteau word, a neat merger of 'breakfast' and 'lunch'. It was coined in Britain in the nineteenth century to describe a meal served the morning after a heavy Saturday night. 'Brunch is cheerful, sociable and inciting,' wrote Guy Beringer in 1895, in an essay for *Hunter's Weekly*. 'It is talk-compelling. It puts you in a good temper, it makes you satisfied with yourself and your fellow beings, it sweeps away the worries and cobwebs of the week.' But brunch really kicked off in twentieth-century America, evolving from an occasional indulgence to placate a hangover, to a fully-fledged fixture of the gastronomic weekend.

Brunch, it is important to point out, is a *substitute* for breakfast and lunch, not an additional meal to be squeezed between the two. (Some enthusiastic eaters might scoff at this suggestion, however. Homer Simpson went one further and claimed that his impressive weight-gain in one episode was down to the fact that he had 'discovered a meal between breakfast and brunch'!)

Another important brunch characteristic is the implicit understanding that the meal contains within its DNA the permission to drink alcohol no matter what time it is served. The hair-of-the-dog qualities of a Bloody Mary or the gentler pick-me-up achieved by a Buck's Fizz (UK) or Mimosa (US) are the acceptable face of morning boozing. (Is it the fresh juice component of these cocktails that makes them feel almost healthy?)

But central to brunch, as to life itself, is the egg. This is such an important constituent of the meal that the repertoire is now groaning: baked, Benedict, boiled, coddled, Connaught, creamed, curried, devilled, Drumkilbo, Fitzpatrick, Florentine, fried, frittata, kedgeree, Muldoon, omelette, poached, rancheros, Scotch, scrambled, steamed and stirred.

In New York City brunch has come into its own and even broken free from the shackles of the weekend. Places such as Shopsin's in Essex Street Market offer scores of egg dishes on a daily basis. Morning queues at West Village brunch spots like Little Owl and Buvette are the norm. And way downtown in TriBeCa, the old-timer Bubby's serves brunch 24 hours a day, 7 days a week. Rather appropriate for the city that never sleeps.

Egg & Soldiers

It is the humour of this dish that makes it so appealing. The eggshell is removed and replaced with a coating of ground almond and sesame seeds so that the sensation of breaking the shell remains, but after dipping your soldiers in the runny yolk you can eat the whole shebang. It is tongue-in-cheek, tasty and it manages to make me smile. Any dish that can do that is all right in my book.

For six:
8 medium eggs
60g ground almonds
1½ teaspoons cayenne
1½ teaspoons sesame seeds
1½ teaspoons smoked paprika
1½ teaspoons fine salt
¾ teaspoon black pepper
100g plain flour
1 litre vegetable oil, for deep frying
Sliced bread for making soldiers, toasted and buttered

Fill a saucepan with cold water and bring to the boil. Gently add six of the eggs in their shells and cook for 5½ minutes exactly and then transfer to iced water (a bowl of water with ice cubes). Once the eggs have completely cooled, peel them, but be very gentle as they will be very soft. Set aside.

Mix together the ground almonds, cayenne, sesame seeds, paprika, salt and pepper.

Now take three bowls. Place the flour in the first, beat the two remaining eggs in the second and put the almond and sesame mix in the third bowl. One by one, dredge the six peeled eggs in the flour and pat off any excess, then dip them in the beaten eggs, shake off any drips, and finally into the almond mixture to coat them well. Set aside at room temperature, not in the fridge.

Heat the vegetable oil in a medium pan to 190°C (or until a cube of bread dropped in the oil turns golden brown in less than a minute). Fry each of the coated eggs for 1 minute, until golden on all sides, then lift out and drain on kitchen paper. Serve hot in egg-cups with toasted, buttered soldiers.

Candied Bacon

This is a preposterous snack that combines the unholy trinity of fat, salt and sugar in one hit. You really can't fit more sin into such a small package; on the other hand, you probably don't need telling how ridiculously tasty it is.

Now, with that warning out of the way, it is only fair to further warn you that this recipe uses a blowtorch. I am aware that this is not a standard bit of kitchen kit, but they're not too expensive these days and they're so handy for a variety of tasks, not least for making that perfect crème brûlée.

For four as a snack:
12 slices of smoked streaky bacon
Maple syrup
Caster sugar

Preheat the oven to 180°C/Gas 4.

Lay a sheet of baking paper on a roasting tray and place the slices of streaky bacon in regimented rows next to each other. Cover with another layer of baking paper and place a second roasting tray on top to create a press. Roast for 15 minutes in the preheated oven. Then lower the temperature to 150°C/Gas 2, remove the upper tray and top layer of baking paper and roast for another 15 minutes. When the bacon looks evenly brown and crisp, remove from the oven and pat dry with kitchen paper.

Allow the rashers to cool for 10 minutes and then brush them with maple syrup. Leave them to dry for 15-20 minutes. Dust with caster sugar and, using a blowtorch, caramelise the sugar on top. Repeat for the reverse. Let them cool again and serve the rigid rashers upright in a short tumbler.

Sage & Chilli Eggs

As a child I had simple tastes. Tea was usually toad-in-the-hole, boil-in-the-bag cod in parsley sauce or fish fingers and peas. But, best of all, on Saturdays we would have egg and chips.

Happily I still feel most enthusiastic about the simplest dishes, such as this variation of eggs-on-toast. Please use the freshest and best eggs you can get. My favourite varieties are Legbar and Burford Brown – the eggs are relatively small but have the deepest orange yolks and a gorgeous depth of flavour.

For four:
Mild olive oil
20g butter
Small handful of sage leaves
8 medium eggs
Flaky sea salt and black pepper
8 slices of ciabatta
1 teaspoon chilli flakes

Place a non-stick saucepan on a low heat. Add a glug of olive oil and the butter. Once the butter has melted, place the sage leaves into the pan and gently fry them until they are crisp. Drain the leaves on kitchen paper.

Crack the eggs individually into the same pan over a low flame and carefully fry them. Season each egg with a small pinch of sea salt and black pepper. At the same time, lightly oil the ciabatta slices and toast both sides under the grill.

Serve the eggs sunny side up on the toasted ciabatta with a small pinch of chilli flakes and arrange the sage leaves on top.

Truffled Egg Toast

This is a mischievous little dish with a killer combination
of crunch, egg, cheese and truffle oil. When served, it looks
sort of like a square fried egg, the Fontina replacing the egg
white, and was inspired by a trip to a tiny but perfectly formed
sandwich shop in the West Village, now sadly closed. The
cooking equipment, so far as I could tell, consisted of six
panini presses. But they rattled out an extensive menu,
including the open truffled egg sandwich to which our
dish is an homage.

The best bread for this, by the way, is one of those square
white farmhouse loaves, which you should buy uncut.

Makes one toast:
1 x 3cm-thick slice of square white bread
80g grated Fontina
2 medium egg yolks
1 teaspoon truffle oil
Flaky sea salt and black pepper

Preheat the oven to 180°C/Gas 4.

Lightly toast the slice of bread on both sides. Place the slice on a baking
tray and, with a very sharp knife, cut a shallow well into the centre of
the bread, about 5cm square. To do this you cut the edges and push
down the centre. Remember, this is a well, not a hole. It is important
that you do not cut all the way through the bread. Distribute the grated
Fontina evenly around the bread rim of the well. Mix the yolks together
and pour them into the well. Place the tray into the preheated oven
and bake for 3–5 minutes, until the cheese melts.

Take the toast out, give the runny yolks a stir, drop the truffle oil evenly
onto the surface and sprinkle over a little salt and pepper.

This really needs to be eaten immediately, while it is still singing,
so to speak.

Lentils, Soft-boiled Egg & Anchovy

There is a magic moment when eating this dish. It comes just after cutting into the soft-boiled egg and letting the runny yolk ooze over the lentils. It's like there's a time-delay on one of the ingredients – it only gets added once you've started to tuck in. The whole dish only really begins to make sense after this moment. I'm a complete sucker for runny eggs.

For six:
200g Castelluccio (or Puy) lentils
1 large carrot, peeled and roughly chopped
4 celery sticks, peeled and roughly chopped
½ fennel bulb, roughly chopped
3 garlic cloves
6 sprigs of rosemary, leaves picked
Extra virgin olive oil
1 large onion, finely diced
1 teaspoon chilli flakes
2 teaspoons fennel seeds, toasted – see page 68 – and ground
Flaky sea salt and black pepper
1 tablespoon Dijon mustard
Small handful of flat parsley leaves, chopped
6 small eggs
12 slices of ciabatta
6 tablespoons Anchovy Dressing – see page 151

Wash the lentils thoroughly and then put them in a large pan of cold water. Bring the pan to the boil, stir once or twice and reduce to a simmer for around 5 minutes. Take off the heat, strain and set aside.

Meanwhile, put the carrot, celery, fennel, garlic and rosemary into a food processor and blend till the vegetables are around the same size as a lentil.

Now place a large frying pan on a low heat with a good glug of olive oil and sweat the onion until soft and translucent, about 8 minutes. Add the vegetables from the processor along with the chilli flakes and ground fennel seeds. Add a little more olive oil if necessary and continue to sweat for about 10 minutes. Add the lentils, stir a few times and then just cover with water and increase the heat to medium. Simmer for 20-25 minutes, stirring occasionally, until the entire mixture has absorbed all the water. The lentils should be al dente. Season with a good pinch of sea salt and black pepper. Add the Dijon mustard and chopped parsley and stir a few times.

While the lentils are simmering, cook the eggs. Bring a large pan of water to the boil, gently add the eggs and cook for 6½ minutes. Immediately transfer to iced water (a bowl of water with ice cubes). Once cooled, peel the eggs and carefully cut them in half. Lightly season with salt and pepper.

Preheat the grill. Brush the ciabatta slices with olive oil and grill on both sides. Top with warmed lentils and soft-boiled egg. Spoon over the anchovy dressing and finish with a drizzle of olive oil.

Leeks, Soft-boiled Egg & Mustard-seed Crumbs

My attitude to leeks has shifted over the years. As a student in Sunderland I would go to Jacky White's market at the end of the day to buy the discounted meats and fruit and veg from stallholders who wanted to go home. Among the smallest turnips and brownest cauliflowers were always several huge leeks, the size of truncheons. Then I would go home and make an enormous batch of stew. Later in life I realised that leeks deserved better.

This dish is as tasty a showcase for them as I know. Because they are cut into batons rather than discs, you should choose the thickest leeks you can find.

For four:
Small hunk of ciabatta (about 100g)
Extra virgin olive oil
1 tablespoon wholegrain mustard
1 tablespoon black mustard seeds
White wine
Flaky sea salt and black pepper
4 large leeks
1 orange, sliced
Small handful of thyme leaves
4 bay leaves
2 garlic cloves, roughly chopped
4 medium eggs
6 tablespoons Lemon Mustard Dressing - see page 146
Small handful of flat parsley leaves, chopped

Preheat the oven to 160°C/Gas 3. Cut the bread into rough cubes of around 2cm and place in a bowl. Coat them with a good glug of olive oil and add the seeded mustard, the mustard seeds, a good splash of white wine and a good pinch of sea salt. Gently massage everything into the bread. Transfer to a baking tray and bake in the preheated oven for about 20 minutes until hard but not coloured. Leave out to cool, then roughly crush to create dishevelled-looking breadcrumbs.

Separate the dark green tops from the white of the leeks, roughly chop and wash them. Put the white leeks to one side. Place the green tops in a pan and cover with water. Bring to the boil and then reduce to a rolling boil. Cook for 30 minutes and then strain and reserve the cooking liquid. Discard the green leek tops.

Preheat the oven to 200°C/Gas 6. Now trim the remaining white parts of the leeks and cut them into sections of about 6-8cm in length; cut these in turn lengthways into batons. Wash them thoroughly and place

in a deep baking tray. Three-quarters cover with the leek stock then add the orange slices, thyme, bay, garlic and a splash of olive oil. Cover with foil and place in the oven for 20 minutes. Remove the foil and cook for a further 20 minutes, until the leeks have some colour.

Meanwhile cook the eggs. Place a pan of water on the stove and bring to the boil. Gently place the eggs into the water and cook for 6½ minutes then transfer to iced water (a bowl of water with ice cubes). Once cooled, peel the eggs and cut them in half. Lightly season with salt and pepper.

Lift the leeks out of the baking tray, discarding all the flavourings, and divide equally between serving plates. Spoon over the dressing and place two egg halves onto each plate. Generously distribute the breadcrumbs around, scatter with the chopped parsley and finish with a drizzle of extra virgin olive oil.

Steak & Eggs

One beautiful Sunday afternoon some years ago, I was sitting with my friend Richard on a terrace table at a Greenwich Village restaurant. The twin towers of the World Trade Center were glistening in the autumn sunshine downtown as we looked south along 6th Avenue.

I asked the waiter for steak and eggs. 'I'm sorry, we don't serve steak and eggs.' Oh really? But I can see here that you have a sirloin steak on the menu. 'Yes we do.' And I can see here that you serve eggs in your brunch section. 'That's right.' But you can't serve me steak and eggs? 'No.' OK, so can I order the sirloin steak, medium rare? 'Sure.' And can I have a side order of eggs, sunny side up? 'No.' Why ever not? 'Because I know what you're gonna do with the eggs.' True story.

For four:
500g sirloin steak
Olive oil
Unsalted butter
8 small eggs
Flaky sea salt and black pepper
Fine salt

Leave the piece of sirloin as it is. Or you could cut it into four even steaks and bash them flat with a wooden mallet or rolling pin so that they are about 10mm thick. Keep the meat out of the fridge for at least 30 minutes before cooking.

Preheat a griddle pan and simultaneously place a non-stick frying pan over a low heat. Add a glug of olive oil and a knob of butter to the latter. Once the butter is melted, fry the eggs gently in batches until the whites are firm but the yolks still runny. Season the eggs with flaky sea salt and black pepper.

Meanwhile, generously season the steak with fine salt and black pepper and lightly brush with olive oil. Place on the smoking hot griddle pan and cook on each side for 30 seconds for the thin steaks, and a few minutes for the larger piece. Transfer the steak to a plate and cover, keeping in a warm place. Let the meat rest for a couple of minutes.

Place two cooked eggs, sunny side up, on each individual steak, season with a small pinch of sea salt and a little twist of black pepper, and serve. Or thinly slice the larger piece and serve alongside the eggs.

Mac & Cheese

Whether you call it Mac & Cheese (US) or Macaroni Cheese (UK), this is one of the world's supreme comfort dishes. President Thomas Jefferson famously served it at a White House banquet in 1802, and it has seen a remarkable return to gastronomic favour in the early years of the twenty-first century. At SPUNTINO we present our Mac & Cheese in individual cast-iron pans, served piping hot straight from the oven. We have held competitions for the longest strings of melted cheese from pan to mouth; the combination of Parmesan, Fontina and mozzarella makes for some seriously stretchy forkfuls.

For six:
250g macaroni pasta
Fine salt
250ml whole milk
450ml double cream
175g grated Parmesan
250g grated mozzarella – the hard, cheap kind
1½ tablespoons Dijon mustard
2 leeks
25g butter
2 garlic cloves, finely chopped
Flaky sea salt and black pepper
75g panko breadcrumbs – see page 62
85g grated Fontina

Bring a large pan of water to a rolling boil, add the pasta and some fine salt, and stir. When the water boils again, turn down to a medium heat and follow the instructions on the packet, usually simmering for around 11 minutes. Drain when al dente.

Once cooled, transfer the drained pasta to a large mixing bowl and add the milk, the double cream, 125g of the Parmesan, half of the mozzarella and the Dijon mustard. Mix together thoroughly and leave to soak for 2 hours.

Meanwhile, trim the leeks by removing and discarding the green tops and the roots, and finely chop. Wash the chopped leeks thoroughly to get rid of any grit. Place a medium pan over a low heat, melt the butter and very gently sweat the leeks with the garlic, 4 large pinches of flaky sea salt and a good pinch of black pepper. After about 10 minutes the leeks will have a translucent, glossy appearance. Take off the heat and leave to cool. Once the leeks have cooled, drain off any lingering fluid and add them to the soaking pasta.

Mix the breadcrumbs with the remaining Parmesan and set aside.

Preheat the oven to 200°C/Gas 6. Add the grated Fontina and the remaining mozzarella to the pasta mixture and combine well. Transfer the mix to a large baking dish or six individual dishes and cover with the breadcrumb and Parmesan mix. Bake in the preheated oven till golden brown and bubbling, for 25–30 minutes if using one large dish, or 15–20 minutes if using individual dishes.

Zucchini, Mint & Ricotta Frittata

Quite often you see frittata described as Italian omelette.
This is inaccurate – there are some important differences
which, being a stickler, I feel duty-bound to point out. The
eggs in a frittata should be beaten very vigorously for several
minutes to aerate the mixture and for a fluffier, thicker result.
The frittata should be cooked at a very low heat and for longer
than an omelette so that the base sets while the top remains
runny. Then the frittata should be finished in an oven so that
the upper layer sets. To serve, frittata should be sliced like
a pie rather than presented whole or folded like an omelette.
Frittata is always served at room temperature or even fridge-
cold, accompanied by salad or 'slaw; omelettes don't respond
well to the cold treatment.

For six:
8 large eggs
250ml whipping cream
Flaky sea salt and black pepper
2 medium zucchini (aka courgettes)
Small handful of mint leaves
Extra virgin olive oil
100g crumbly ricotta (or feta)

Preheat the oven to 180°C/Gas 4. Crack the eggs into a mixing bowl and
add the cream, a large pinch of sea salt and a few twists of black pepper.
Whisk really well for a minute or two.

Trim the ends off the zucchini, wash them thoroughly and pat dry.
Coarsely grate the zucchini, chop the mint, and add both to the egg mix.

Place a 20-25cm non-stick frying pan on a low to medium heat and
add a glug of olive oil. Pour in the egg mix and use a spatula to move
it around, then let it cook gently until it starts to set, after 5-10 minutes.
Gently separate the sides from the edges of the frying pan with the
spatula. If you shake the pan, the whole frittata should move
independently but the top should still be runny.

Remove the pan from the heat and carefully slide the frittata out of the
pan and onto a baking tray. (If your pan has an ovenproof handle, you
could skip this step.) Scatter chunks of ricotta on top and put the tray
(or the frying pan) into the oven for 10 minutes until the surface has set
and has taken on a golden brown colour. Remove the frittata, allow it
to cool, and then serve or refrigerate for later. It should keep for a day
in the fridge.

West Village, Greenwich Village, Meatpacking District

Buvette

About 2.5 miles
1 hour walking plus pit stops
Best time of day: 10am
Subway: Christopher Street-Sheridan Square, L train

Warning: Opening times change and places come and go. Please check availability before heading to any specific eating place.

In my mind's eye, this walk starts on a Sunday morning. It is March or April, the sun is shining, the sky has that deep blue hue, yet there is a pleasant, crisp chill in the air.

And what better way to start Sunday morning than with a good coffee and a plate of smoked salmon and scrambled eggs? As you climb the steps at the Christopher Street-Sheridan Square subway station, here's hoping into bright sunlight, you should head south west along Grove Street to Buvette (42 Grove St between Bleecker and Bedford). This tiny but incredibly popular brunch spot is styled like a quirky Parisian café – no coincidence, there is one in Paris too. For a restaurateur, here is a remarkable lesson in economy of design; the tiniest tables and cosiest bar stools help squeeze as many people in as possible. The plates are smaller than you would find elsewhere, and you'll notice that the pastries have been scaled down to fit onto them. It is the Lilliput of restaurants. If you can manoeuvre yourself to get a view of the bar, watch how the scrambled eggs are prepared – the eggs are cracked into a jug, then cooked using the steamer from an espresso machine. Ingenious.

With a bit of luck you will have saved some room for your next breakfast snack, which is just moments away. Turn left out of Buvette and walk half a block to the corner of Grove and Bedford Streets where you will find the Little Owl (90 Bedford St). Here you can enjoy your next course, what my daughters call 'breakfast pudding': a short stack of pancakes and maple syrup. The Little Owl has been a principal player on the New York brunch scene for as long as I can remember and yet still has a friendly, neighbourhood attitude. Two blocks south, across the road between Commerce and Morton Streets, you will find the narrowest house in New York at 75½ Bedford Street, once home to the poet Edna St Vincent Millay, best known for the poem 'First Fig':

Little Owl

Murray's Cheese

Matt Uvanov's Guitar Shop

My candle burns at both ends;
It will not last the night;
But ah, my foes, and oh, my friends –
It gives a lovely light!

Continuing south along Bedford you will notice how peaceful the tree-lined streets are, such a contrast to the sirens and concrete beyond. Turn left onto Carmine Street and stroll two short blocks until you hit 6th Avenue, also known as Avenue of the Americas. Two more short blocks north turning right onto West 4th Street, then one more block will bring you to Washington Square Park. Here you can take a stroll around the square, which on a warm sunny morning will be teeming with joggers, yoga classes, cute pugs, drug casualties, eccentrics and the resident chess hustlers in the south-west corner. If chess is your thing, you can sit down at a table and let one of these experts humiliate you for a few dollars. If not, spend a little time watching – you want to build up an appetite for lunch.

Head back the way you came on West 4th Street and take the left turn immediately after 6th Avenue. This is Cornelia Street and will take you straight onto Bleecker Street.

Opposite the end of Cornelia is Murray's Cheese (254 Bleecker St). This store has been supplying cheeses to the Village since the 1940s and is an Aladdin's cave of fermented dairy goods from near and far – Moses Sleeper from Vermont, Hudson Red from New York State, Truffle Tremor from California among them. It's a good place, should you feel the urge, to pick up a small olive-wood cheese board or a carved maple butter spatula.

Next door is Faicco's (260 Bleecker St), another evocative 1940s stalwart, selling 'The Finest Sausage & Italian Specialties', which is also worth a browse.

Continue north along Bleecker, maybe picking up a few plectrums (plectra?) at Matt Uvanov's Guitar Shop (273 Bleecker St) before crossing

Washington Square Park

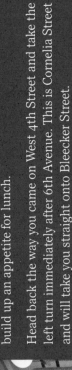

Faicco's

John's Pizzeria

Magnolia Bakery

the road to John's Pizzeria (278 Bleecker St), your stop for a swift lunch. The best room to sit in is the first, with a view of the brick-built oven and a seat in one of the shonky plywood booths carved with thousands of names from decades of condoned graffiti. The pizza (or 'pie' as the locals call it) is huge; you may want to consider sharing.

After lunch, turn left outside John's and continue at a leisurely pace northwards along Bleecker. The street is still populated by an encouraging number of independent record shops, stationers and bookstores. One of my favourite shops is on the right, just before 7th Avenue. O Ottomanelli & Sons (285 Bleecker St) is a wonderfully evocative butcher's with whole sides of lamb hanging in the window. The shopfront is a real beauty, too.

When you are almost at the end of Bleecker Street, where it meets West 11th, you will find Magnolia Bakery (401 Bleecker St). This is probably the most famous cake shop in all New York, championed by the fictitious Carrie Bradshaw in *Sex and the City*. The cupcakes are, as you would expect, very good, with lashings of butter icing. The store has undeniable charm, too, feeling more like a suburban English tea-room than a Manhattan bakery.

At the end of Bleecker Street, cross 8th Avenue onto Hudson Street where you should head north, sticking to the right-hand side of the road. Between Jane and Horatio you will pass Myers of Keswick (634 Hudson St), a quirky grocery store specialising in British produce. If you do pop inside for a jar of Marmite or a packet of Tunnock's Caramel Wafers, send my regards to Molly, the shop's cat. Molly was quite dramatically rescued from the gap between two buildings a few years ago; her story made international television news.

Continuing north another block, take the left turn onto Gansevoort Street and head towards the Hudson River. Just before you get there you will hit the High Line, a disused raised freight railway that has been turned into an astonishingly lovely public park. Climb the steps and, depending on the crowds, wander around for a while to take in the view.

O. OTTOMANELLI & SONS

O Ottomanelli & Sons

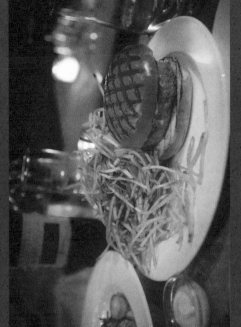

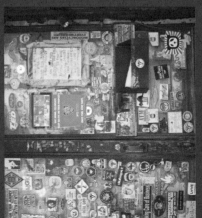

Spotted Pig

Back down on Washington Street you are now in the heart of the Meatpacking District. Until relatively recently, this area was a working hub and mornings would see the wide streets crammed with lorries loading and unloading their meaty cargoes. The gentrification into a high-end retail zone has been swift. But there are still pockets of the old meatpacking industry. In particular, on Washington between Little West 12th and Gansevoort, there is a stubborn, die-hard contingent of the old guard who still trade and proudly paint their names large on steel fascia: J T JOBBAGY INC, LOUIS ZUCKER & CO, JOHN W WILLIAMS INC and WEICHEL BEEF CO.

It's probably time for a beer. On the corner of West 13th Street you'll find Hogs & Heifers (859 Washington St). The red neon sign is almost completely obscured by the grime on the window, the front door has all but disappeared under layers of stickers and beer labels, the female bartenders are famously rude, the ceiling is decorated with hundreds of bras, the music is deafeningly loud and the bathrooms are not for the faint-hearted, but you can imagine the place being very popular with testosterone-fuelled meatpackers, blowing off steam after a hard shift hauling ox carcasses.

The speed with which you exit Hogs & Heifers will depend on how much of that Coyote Ugly experience you have an appetite for. Turn left and head south down Washington Street. This is a pleasant stroll with the Freedom Tower always clearly in your sights in the distance.

As you continue south down Washington, look up at the buildings on your right, specifically between Bethune and Bank Streets, above Westbeth Artists' Housing at 744 Washington. You will notice a remnant of the High Line's derelict elevated railway rusting away. At West 11th turn left and walk one more block to the corner of Greenwich Street. Here you will find the Spotted Pig (314 W. 11th St), the city's most famous gastropub, owned and run by two of my food heroes, April Bloomfield and Ken Friedman. Here you should stay for a while, reflect on your village walk, enjoy the buzz, share a plate of April's delicious gnudi, and plan where you're going to go for dinner.

Myers of Keswick

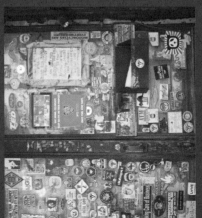

Hogs & Heifers

Spuntini & Toasts

I prefer menus that are under-described. Adjectives get in the way. Ernest Hemingway said that if a prose writer understands his subject well enough, he can leave out things he knows the reader will intuit. He compares good writing to an iceberg – only one eighth is visible.

Now I would not dare to compare menu prose to Nobel-prize-winning literature but, still, our customers do not need to be told that something is 'juicy', 'fresh', 'delicious', 'delicate' or 'fragrant'. They can be the judges of that. Nor do I like overblown names for simple foods. The word 'toast' is blunt, yes. Inelegant, possibly. But that's what it is.

There is a satisfying connection between economy in description and simplicity in the execution of the dishes that follow. They are all designed to be eaten before your meal proper as bar snacks, the sort of food that is perfect to munch while you enjoy a cocktail or two. In fact many of them contain those essential elements (salt, fat, strong flavours) that go so well with a Martini or a Negroni. But if you wanted to create a meal entirely from this section, that's fine too. Often at SPUNTINO our diners will order a succession of drinks and simply ask to be kept topped-up on the snack front. If this is your game plan I recommend that you include several of the toasts. They are particularly fortifying.

Salt Cod Toast

I have had a bit of a love affair with salt cod ever since
first tasting it in a humble wine bar in Venice nearly twenty
years ago. Infused with garlic and olive oil and beaten into
submission, salt cod undergoes a sublime transformation
into the classic *baccalà mantecato*. This little *crostino* definitely
shares DNA with that inspired taste of the sea, but with less
of the sheer elbow grease required for a true Venetian *baccalà*.

For eight:
500g salt cod fillet
1 onion, roughly chopped
2 celery sticks, cut in half
4 bay leaves
1 large floury potato
Fine salt and black pepper
2 garlic cloves, finely chopped
250ml extra virgin olive oil
150ml whole milk
16 slices of ciabatta

Wash the salt cod in a bowl of cold water several times, refreshing the
water each time. Cut in half and then in half again. Place in a saucepan
with the onion, celery and bay and just cover with water, placing a lid
over the top. Bring to the boil, then reduce to a simmer, and cook for
20 minutes or more, until the cod is easy to flake but still holding its
shape. Gently lift it out of the water. Keep about 120ml of the cooking
liquid and discard the remainder, along with the flavourings.

Meanwhile wash the potato and place it in a small pan, cover with cold
water and add a pinch of salt. Bring to the boil, then reduce the heat a
little. Cook it until just tender and you can pierce it easily with the tip of
a sharp knife. Once cool enough to handle, peel and cut into small pieces.

Break up the cod with your hands, removing any bones and skin. Place
both the potato and the cod into a mixer and beat on a slow speed
using the paddle attachment. Once the mixture has combined, add the
garlic and half the oil, and gradually increase the speed to high, whipping
the fish mixture to lighten it. Reduce to medium and incorporate most
of the remaining oil and the milk gradually, then whip at high speed
again. At this point the whipped cod should be smooth and fluffy, almost
like mashed potatoes. If it is very dense, you can thin it with the cooking
liquid you have reserved (but be careful: too much fishy water will make
it too salty). Finally, season with two large pinches of black pepper.

Now place a heavy-based griddle pan over a medium to high heat.
Lightly brush the bread slices with olive oil and grill on both sides to
char them slightly. Generously top with salt cod, drizzle a little more
olive oil over the top and serve.

Smoked Cod Roe Toast

Cod roe has a depth of flavour that you just don't get from the flesh of the fish that produces it. As a student I first came across roe in the guise of taramasalata: shockingly ointment-pink in colour and sold in tubs from the supermarket. Artificial as it was, it hit the mark. Although the quality of mass-produced taramasalata has improved, you don't need to buy it since it is so simple to make something so much better. You can buy whole smoked roes vacuum-packed at most supermarkets. They are rather improbably shaped, like large cartoon love hearts.

For six:
250g smoked cod roe
50g stale (day-old) white bread
¾ teaspoon cayenne
½ tablespoon lemon juice
1 small garlic clove, finely chopped
Pinch of black pepper
Extra virgin olive oil
Flaky sea salt
12 slices of ciabatta
¼ Pickled Cucumber – in the recipe for Lamb Meatball Slider,
        see page 162 – very thinly sliced

Remove and discard the skin from the cod roe and break the roe into chunks. Soak the stale white bread in cold water for a couple of minutes, then remove the bread and gently squeeze out the excess water (reserve the liquid). Place the bread into a food processor with the roe, cayenne, lemon juice, chopped garlic and pepper. Process until smooth and, with the motor still going, add 150ml of the olive oil in a steady stream. If necessary, you can loosen the mixture a little by adding some of the water that the bread was soaked in. Taste and season with salt if needed.

Now place a heavy-based griddle pan over a medium heat. Lightly coat the sliced ciabatta with a few brushes of olive oil and grill for about 1 minute per side, creating nice char marks. Liberally top with cod roe, then with pickled cucumber slices, and serve immediately.

Ricotta, Redcurrant & Fennel Toast

Ricotta is a curd cheese that proves its credentials for me every time I taste it. Made from sheep's milk, it has a subtle tang and a delicate texture. Here its silkiness joyfully contrasts with the pop from the redcurrants and the crunch from the fennel.

For four:
200g ricotta
Flaky sea salt and black pepper
20ml whole milk
Extra virgin olive oil
½ fennel bulb, thinly sliced
A few sprigs of mint, leaves picked and chopped
75g redcurrants, picked and washed
1-2 tablespoons Lemon Mustard Dressing - see page 146
½ baguette
1 garlic clove, peeled and halved

Drain any liquid from the ricotta and place the cheese in the small bowl of a food processor along with a large pinch of flaky salt and a few twists of black pepper. Pulse briefly, then with the motor running, add the milk and a glug of olive oil. You want the ricotta to be smooth and spreadable.

Place the fennel, mint and redcurrants into a mixing bowl and coat with a tablespoon or so of the dressing.

Put a heavy-based griddle pan on a medium to high heat and cut the baguette at an angle into eight slices. Lightly brush the bread with olive oil and grill on both sides. Rub with garlic and generously spoon on the whipped ricotta. Top with some of the fennel and redcurrant salad and serve immediately.

Duck Liver & Onion Jam Crostini

It baffles me that duck livers aren't more popular. They have an earthiness, a gravitas even, that chicken livers lack, and are delicious in a pâté or terrine. This simple preparation marries them with sweet onion jam to lovely effect.

For six to eight:
1 onion, sliced
1 garlic clove, finely chopped
6 sage leaves, finely chopped
Extra virgin olive oil
Flaky sea salt and black pepper
100ml port
Splash of sherry vinegar
250g duck livers, sinews removed
250g unsalted butter, melted
12-16 slices of ciabatta

For the onion jam:
6 red onions, finely sliced
Extra virgin olive oil
2 garlic cloves, finely chopped
50g soft dark brown sugar
50ml red wine vinegar

To make the jam, place the sliced red onions in a heavy-based saucepan over a medium heat with a good glug of olive oil, a good few pinches of flaky sea salt and a good pinch of black pepper, and stir so that the onions don't stick to the bottom of the pan or change colour. Once they are completely soft, after about 10-15 minutes, add the garlic, sugar and vinegar and sweat for another 10 minutes until the vinegar has evaporated. Leave the onions to cool to room temperature.

To start the pâté, put the sliced onion, garlic and sage in a heavy-based saucepan on a medium heat with a good glug of olive oil, season with a good pinch each of salt and pepper and sweat until the onion is soft but has not changed colour, about 10-12 minutes. Add the port and continue cooking to reduce it until syrupy and then add the sherry vinegar and cook for a few minutes more. Tip into the bowl of a food processor.

In the same pan heat a good glug of olive oil over a medium heat. Season the duck livers and fry until brown, making sure they are still pink in the middle, no more than 4 minutes. Remove from the heat.

Place the duck livers in the food processor with the cooked onions and process until smooth. With the motor still running, very slowly trickle in the melted butter until fully incorporated. Push through a coarse sieve into a bowl, and set aside to cool, then chill until firm.

When ready to serve, place a heavy-based griddle pan over a medium heat. Lightly coat the sliced bread with a few brushes of olive oil and grill on both sides until slightly charred. Spread with duck liver and serve with a dollop of onion jam on top.

Mozzarella & Cavolo Nero Crostini

When it is in season, cavolo nero is one of my hero ingredients. Its deep, dark green colour and its long crinkled leaves are incredibly glamorous, and it is surprisingly versatile. Florence Knight, one of my favourite chefs, picks the smallest, most delicate raw leaves and tosses them in a delightful anchovy dressing with bread fried in butter. Delicious.

This recipe specifies a swift blanch; you really mustn't overcook the cavolo nero, otherwise it loses much of its flavour and many of its nutrients too.

For four:
1 bunch of cavolo nero, about 200g, stems removed
3 garlic cloves
Good handful of grated Parmesan, about 20g
Flaky sea salt and black pepper
Extra virgin olive oil
Juice of 1 lemon
8 slices of ciabatta
2 x 125g balls of buffalo mozzarella, at room temperature

Place a pan of salted water over a high heat. Cut the cavolo nero into 2cm strips. Once the water has come to the boil, add the cavolo nero and, when the water comes back to the boil, blanch for 2 minutes. Drain and, when cool enough to handle, squeeze out the excess liquid.

Transfer the cavolo nero to the small bowl of a food processor. Add two of the garlic cloves, the Parmesan and some salt and pepper, and whizz to a purée. With the motor still going slowly add 100ml of the olive oil, then transfer to a mixing bowl and fold in the lemon juice.

Now place a heavy-based griddle pan over a medium heat. Lightly coat the sliced bread with a few brushes of olive oil and grill on both sides until lightly charred. Halve the remaining garlic clove and rub over the hot grilled bread. Top with broken-up pieces of mozzarella and a generous amount of the cavolo nero purée. Serve immediately.

Braised Octopus & Chickpea Toast

Don't be scared of octopuses. They are strange creatures, granted, and a lot of people are put off by their otherworldliness, their shape-shifting abilities and their unpredictable tentacles, but when they're washed up on the fishmonger's slab, you have nothing to fear. Octopus flesh is often described as rubbery, but cooked properly it can be soft, yielding and even silky. Combining it here with chickpeas results in a lovely, smoky flavour and a good, earthy texture.

Ask the fishmonger to clean the beast and remove the beak, eyes and mush inside the head for you.

For six:
1 medium octopus, cleaned
Fine sea salt
Handful of flat parsley, chopped (keep the stalks)
3 celery sticks, peeled and sliced (keep the peelings)
1 small fennel bulb, thinly sliced (keep the fronds)
2 carrots, chopped
3 small onions, 2 sliced, 1 chopped
Extra virgin olive oil
4 garlic cloves, 3 finely chopped, 1 whole
1g saffron strands
200g cooked chickpeas (you could use tinned,
     drain and rinse them first)
12 slices of ciabatta
Pinch of paprika

Place the octopus in a suitably sized saucepan, and cover with water. Add some fine salt, along with the parsley stalks, celery peelings, fennel fronds, chopped carrot and chopped onion. Bring to the boil, then reduce to a simmer and cook for 30 minutes, or until tender. Remove the octopus from the water and drain. Discard the cooking water and flavourings.

Meanwhile pour 75ml of the olive oil into a heavy-based saucepan and add the sliced onion, celery and fennel, and the chopped garlic. Sweat on a low heat until very soft, about 25 minutes, stirring every so often.

Once the octopus has cooled enough to handle, slice on an angle into 2.5cm pieces and add to the pan with the vegetables, along with the saffron, the cooked chickpeas and a glug or two of olive oil, if needed.

Mix together well, season and continue to cook for 5 minutes or until everything is warmed through. Just before serving turn the chopped parsley through the mixture.

Now place a heavy-based griddle pan over a medium heat. Lightly coat the sliced bread with a few brushes of olive oil and grill on both sides until slightly charred. Halve the remaining garlic clove, and rub over both sides of the hot grilled bread. Generously top with braised octopus and chickpeas, sprinkle with paprika, and serve immediately.

Croque Monsieur

I once had a rather good croque monsieur at Harry's Bar in Venice. It was a miserable, rainy day and I was in the mood for a Martini. I fancied something hot and salty to accompany the cocktail and this fitted the bill. In many ways it is the perfect snack: salty ham, melted cheese and carbohydrate. Three nutritional no-nos in one package. The best bread for this dish is a blue-collar sliced white.

For six:
300g Gruyère cheese, grated
1 medium egg yolk
1 tablespoon double cream
1 tablespoon Worcestershire sauce
1½ teaspoons Dijon mustard
Good pinch each of flaky sea salt and black pepper
1 teaspoon cayenne
6 thick slices of white bread, crusts off
3 thick slices of good sandwich ham
Large knob of butter
Olive oil

In a large bowl, thoroughly mix the cheese, egg yolk, cream, Worcestershire sauce, mustard, salt, pepper and cayenne until smooth. Spread the cheese mixture evenly over one side of all six slices of bread. Lay a slice of ham on three of the slices and put the remaining bread slices on top, cheese topping down, so that you are left with three square sandwiches.

Place a heavy-based frying pan on a medium to low heat and melt the butter, adding a good glug of olive oil. When the butter and oil start to bubble, fry each sandwich on both sides until golden brown. Drain on kitchen paper to remove excess grease.

Using a very sharp knife, cut the sandwiches in half lengthways to create rectangles and wrap in sandwich paper. Serve while hot.

Ham & Cheese Crocchette

Croquettes get a bad rap. Their reputation is not helped
by the economy versions that lurk in the freezer cabinets
of supermarkets. Yuck. These croquettes are a far superior
model, torpedoes of cheesy, hammy loveliness.

Panko is a type of breadcrumb used as a crisp coating
in Japanese deep frying: the flaky crumbs are made from
bread without crusts, and they do not absorb as much fat
as traditional crumbs. You can find it in supermarkets.

For four (makes about twenty crocchette):
Olive oil
50g unsalted butter
100g prosciutto, roughly chopped
80g plain flour
400ml hot milk
40g Pecorino, grated
Flaky sea salt and black pepper
2 medium eggs, beaten
100g panko breadcrumbs – see above
1 litre vegetable oil, for deep frying

Heat a good splash of olive oil and the butter in a heavy-based saucepan
over a medium heat. When the butter has melted, add the prosciutto
and cook until the ham fat has melted. Turn down the heat and
gradually stir in half the flour until it is absorbed. Now gradually stir in
the hot milk, beating until you have a paste. Cook for 10 minutes until
the mixture is smooth, stirring now and then. Fold in the Pecorino,
check the seasoning, and spread on a tray to cool.

Once cooled, roll the mixture out into cylinders of roughly 7cm x 2cm.
Now take three bowls. Place the remaining flour in the first, the beaten
eggs in the second and the breadcrumbs in the third bowl. One by one,
dredge the croquettes in the flour and pat off any excess, then dip them
in the egg wash, shake off any drips, and finally into the breadcrumbs
to coat them well. Set aside at room temperature, not in the fridge.

Heat the vegetable oil in a medium pan to 190°C (or until a cube of
bread dropped in the oil turns golden brown in less than a minute).
Now fry the croquettes in batches, until golden brown on all sides,
about 2–3 minutes. Lift out and drain on kitchen paper. Serve hot,
sprinkled with a little flaky sea salt.

Cauliflower & Gorgonzola Crocchette

Nowadays I find cauliflower such a versatile vegetable, yet childhood memories of it boiled to the point of disintegration make me feel slightly traumatised. It deserves so much better than the treatment it is sometimes given.

Here, combined with Gorgonzola Dolce – Dolcelatte – it takes on such a creamy, velvety texture that it is almost possible to forget that childhood trauma.

For six (makes about twenty-four crocchette):
1 medium cauliflower
Fine salt
Flaky sea salt and black pepper
Extra virgin olive oil
150g unsalted butter
500ml whole milk
150g plain flour, plus 100g for coating
200g Dolcelatte, broken into pieces
2 teaspoons fine salt
4 medium eggs, beaten
150g panko breadcrumbs – see page 62
1 litre vegetable oil, for deep frying

Preheat the oven to 180°C/Gas 4. Heat a large pan of water over a high heat, and add some fine salt. Meanwhile cut the cauliflower into small pieces, and once the water has come to the boil add the cauliflower to blanch for 4 minutes. Drain and put the florets on a baking tray with a good pinch of flaky sea salt, a good twist of ground black pepper and a generous glug of olive oil. Cover with foil and place in the preheated oven for 10–15 minutes, or until tender. Remove from the oven, allow to cool a little, then place in a food processor and blend.

Melt the butter in a heavy-based saucepan over a medium heat. In another pan gently heat the milk. Once the butter has melted, slowly start adding the 150g flour, stirring with a wooden spoon to make sure there are no lumps. Gradually add the hot milk in stages, stirring all the while. Cook for a further 5–10 minutes until the mixture has thickened and is smooth. Add the broken-up pieces of Dolcelatte and a good few pinches each of flaky sea salt and black pepper. Finally fold in the puréed cauliflower, and lay out on a tray to cool down.

Once the mixture has cooled you can have some fun rolling it into small cylindrical croquettes. Now take three bowls. Place the 100g coating flour in the first with the fine salt, the beaten eggs in the second and the breadcrumbs in the third bowl. One by one, dredge the croquettes in the flour and pat off any excess, then dip them in the egg wash, shake off any drips, and finally into the breadcrumbs to coat them well. Set aside at room temperature, not in the fridge.

Heat the vegetable oil in a medium pan to 190°C (or until a cube of bread dropped in the oil turns golden brown in less than a minute). Fry the croquettes, in batches, for 1–2 minutes or until golden brown, lift out and drain on kitchen paper. Serve hot.

Fried Stuffed Green Olives

This is a devious dish, which draws you in with a promise of savoury loveliness and then delivers far more than you were ever expecting. It's perfect with cocktails like Manhattans, Martinis and Sours. If these olives don't sharpen your appetite and get your juices going, nothing will.

It may sound very fiddly to attempt to stuff something so small as an olive, but these little snacks are worth the effort. Try to get hold of the largest olives you can; crunchy Green Queens from Sicily are particularly good. You will need a piping bag with a narrow nozzle to make these.

For four:
100g brown anchovies in oil (drained weight but save the oil)
Small handful of sage leaves
25g grated Parmesan
Juice of ½ lemon
1 garlic clove, finely chopped
½ teaspoon black pepper
100g pitted large green olives
200g plain flour
4 medium eggs, beaten
200g panko breadcrumbs – see page 62
1 litre vegetable oil, for deep frying

Combine the anchovies, sage, Parmesan, lemon juice, garlic and pepper in a blender and whizz to a paste. Use the retained anchovy oil to loosen the mixture if necessary.

Put the anchovy mix into a piping bag fitted with a narrow nozzle, push the nozzle into a pitted olive and, pressing hard on the bag, squeeze the mix into the olive. You may need to experiment to get the size right. Once the olives have all been stuffed, set aside.

Now take three bowls. Place the flour in the first, the beaten eggs in the second and the breadcrumbs in the third bowl. One by one, roll the stuffed olives in the flour, pat off any excess, then dip them in the egg wash, shake off any drips, and finally into the breadcrumbs to coat them well. Set aside at room temperature, not in the fridge.

Heat the vegetable oil in a medium pan to 190°C (or until a cube of bread dropped in the oil turns golden brown in less than a minute). Now fry the olives, in batches, until golden brown on all sides, lift out and drain on kitchen paper. Serve hot.

Eggplant Chips with Fennel Yoghurt

This has been on the menu at SPUNTINO since day one and is a much-requested recipe. For me, it's a dish about contrasts. The hot eggplant chips versus the cool yoghurt. The crunchy sesame coating versus the soft centre. The smoky flavour of the eggplant versus the aniseed tang of the fennel. You can have fun with the presentation of this dish too, by using a shot glass for the fennel yoghurt and then stacking the chips around or to the side.

For six to eight:
2 teaspoons coriander seeds
2 teaspoons fennel seeds
2 eggplants (aka aubergines)
100g plain flour
1 teaspoon fine salt
½ teaspoon black pepper
3-4 medium eggs
150g panko breadcrumbs - see page 62
2 teaspoons sesame seeds
1 litre vegetable oil, for deep frying

For the fennel yoghurt:
1 teaspoon coriander seeds
1 teaspoon fennel seeds
125g mayonnaise
200g plain Greek-style yoghurt
1 teaspoon lemon juice
Large pinch of flaky sea salt
Pinch of black pepper

First of all, toast the coriander and fennel seeds for both the aubergine and the yoghurt. Put them all - 3 teaspoons of each - in a non-stick frying pan and dry fry over a medium heat for a few minutes, until you can smell their spiciness. Do keep an eye on them, as they can easily burn. Remove from the heat, then grind in a pestle and mortar.

Now make the fennel yoghurt. Take 2 teaspoons of the ground seeds and combine with the rest of the fennel yoghurt ingredients. Put it in the fridge.

Cut the eggplant into thick 10cm-long chips.

Now take three bowls. Mix the flour, salt and pepper in the first. In the second bowl, beat the eggs. Mix together the breadcrumbs,

the remaining ground coriander and fennel seeds and the sesame seeds in the third bowl. Dip the eggplant chips in the flour, coating well, shake off any excess and then place in the egg wash, shaking off any drips, and then coat well with the breadcrumbs. Set aside at room temperature, not in the fridge, if not cooking straightaway.

Heat the vegetable oil in a medium pan to 190°C (or until a cube of bread dropped in the oil turns golden brown in less than a minute). Now fry the coated eggplant chips, in batches, for 2–3 minutes or until golden brown. Lift out, drain on kitchen paper and sprinkle with a little salt. Serve hot with the chilled fennel yoghurt.

Fried Whitebait & Dill

In my experience, whitebait often gets a bad press. Perhaps
it is because these skinny little babies of the herring and
sprat family are considered inelegant and too commonplace.
Whitebait is certainly very plentiful around the British coast
and I remember polishing off plate after plate of them as
a child on summer holidays in Southend-on-Sea.

The preparation here is so simple; you just need to
rinse the fish in running cold water, no gutting or scaling
required. Choose the smallest whitebait you can find.

For four:
200g plain flour
Fine salt and black pepper
1 litre vegetable oil, for deep frying
500g whitebait
1 lemon, cut into wedges

For the dill dip:
Small handful of dill fronds, chopped – with a few fronds reserved
        for garnish
Juice of 1 lemon
1 garlic clove, finely chopped
60ml vegetable oil
80ml Mayonnaise – see page 152

For the dip, place the dill, lemon juice, garlic and vegetable oil in a
blender and mix until well combined. Whisk this into the mayonnaise
and set aside.

Place the flour in a bowl and add a teaspoon of fine salt and a good
pinch of black pepper. Heat the vegetable oil in a medium pan to 190°C
(or until a cube of bread dropped in the oil turns golden brown in less
than a minute).

Coat the whitebait in the flour, then deep fry for a couple of minutes.
Drain on kitchen paper and season with some more fine salt.

Transfer to a large plate, sprinkle with any extra dill fronds, and
serve with a generous dollop of the dill dip and lemon wedges.

Fried Rice Balls

These are called *arancini* in Italian, literally meaning 'little oranges', which is what these tasty rice balls should (sort of) look like when they are done, the breadcrumb coating having taken on a lovely golden hue.

You can, incidentally, make them from leftover risotto – just follow the recipe from the instruction to roll the mixture into balls.

For eight (makes twenty-four balls):
Olive oil
1 onion, finely diced
1 garlic clove, finely chopped
Flaky sea salt and black pepper
100g carnaroli rice
100ml white wine
500ml vegetable stock, hot
100g finely grated Parmesan
Juice and finely grated zest of 1 lemon
Large knob of butter
6 medium eggs
250g grated block mozzarella – the hard, cheap kind
Small handful of lovage leaves, finely chopped
    (you could use celery leaves, oregano or basil instead)
Handful of chives, finely chopped
125g plain flour
Fine salt
125g panko breadcrumbs – see page 62
1 litre vegetable oil, for deep frying

Put a good glug of olive oil in heavy-based saucepan over a low heat and add the onion and garlic with a good pinch each of flaky salt and black pepper. Sauté until the onion is soft and translucent, about 10 minutes.

Turn up the heat a little, add the rice and stir for about 1 minute to coat every grain well. Add the wine and cook until it has almost disappeared, then add two big ladles of the hot vegetable stock and stir a couple of times until it has been completely absorbed. Keep adding the stock, slowly and a little at a time, stirring, until the rice is al dente and there is no liquid left.

Add the Parmesan, lemon juice and butter, and stir well to combine. Beat three of the eggs in a bowl, and add them, plus half of the grated mozzarella, to the rice. Mix quickly so that the eggs don't scramble. Check the seasoning.

Transfer to a tray, leave to cool completely and then add the lemon zest, chopped herbs and the remainder of the grated mozzarella.

When the rice is completely cold, roll the mixture into balls (a little smaller than a golf ball) and lay out on a baking tray. Now take three bowls. Place the flour and a very good pinch of fine salt in the first, beat the remaining three eggs in the second, and place the breadcrumbs in the third bowl. Firstly dredge the little balls in the flour, and shake off any excess, then dip them in the beaten eggs, and shake off any drips, and lastly coat them in the breadcrumbs. Continue until all the balls are coated, then set aside at room temperature, not in the fridge.

Heat the vegetable oil in a medium pan to 190°C (or until a cube of bread dropped in the oil turns golden brown in less than a minute). Now deep fry the coated rice balls, in batches, until golden brown on all sides, about 4-5 minutes. Lift out and drain on kitchen paper. Serve hot on their own or with a dollop of aïoli, garlicky mayonnaise (see page 152).

Spiced Nuts

Here is a simple way to improve a bowl of boring nuts.
Five minutes in the oven and a dusting of spices make
all the difference in terms of flavour and texture, and if
you time things right you can be serving them warm as
your guests sip their first cocktail.

For four:
10g rosemary leaves
Olive oil
100g pecan nuts
100g raw almonds
100g hazelnuts, skinned
Caster sugar
Fine salt and black pepper
10g cayenne

Preheat the oven to 160°C/Gas 3.

Scatter the rosemary leaves over a baking tray and place in the oven
for 10 minutes or so to dry out. Once cooled, use a pestle and mortar
to pulverise the rosemary into a fine dust.

Turn the oven up to 180°C/Gas 4. In a bowl, lightly oil the nuts and
coat them with a good sprinkle of sugar, a generous pinch each of salt
and pepper and the cayenne. Place on the baking tray and roast in the
oven for 5 minutes till golden. Toss with the rosemary powder while
still hot, and serve.

Pickles

Pickles are a great way to start the ball rolling before a meal.
They are crunchy and piquant, with just the right balance
between sweet and sour. In fact, a good pickle is like an
appetite catalyst, setting up your taste buds for more serious
work. There are times, however, when I visit the restaurant
and eat a plate of pickles and nothing else.

I always like to serve a few different pickles on a pretty
plate – at SPUNTINO we use silver goblets – with a glass
of prosecco. They can be eaten as a snack, or a starter,
and we use them as ingredients in other recipes. Keep
them no longer than a week.

Basic vinegar pickling brine

900ml boiling water
1 litre white wine vinegar or cider vinegar
900g caster sugar
60g coarse sea salt

Combine the water and vinegar, then add the sugar and salt, stirring
until they have dissolved. This brine keeps forever - just use the
quantity required and save the rest for next time. Use the brine hot
or cold according to the individual recipes, and check whether white
wine or cider vinegar is required.

Beetroot

4 medium beetroots, peeled and halved
100g fresh horseradish
White wine vinegar pickling brine, hot

Cut the beetroot halves into semi-circles about 5mm thick, wash them
thoroughly and set aside. Now peel the horseradish and cut into small
chunks. Pack both the beetroot and horseradish into a Kilner jar and
cover with hot brine. Leave for three days before using.

Fennel

4 medium fennel bulbs
6 star anise
White wine vinegar pickling brine, hot

Trim the fennel of its feathery fronds, then cut into bite-sized batons.
Place the fennel and star anise in a Kilner jar and cover with hot brine.
Leave for three days before using.

Rhubarb

4 sticks of rhubarb
2 teaspoons juniper berries
4 bay leaves
White wine vinegar pickling brine, cold

Trim the ends off the rhubarb and cut the sticks into bite-sized batons.
Wash thoroughly. Place in a Kilner jar with the juniper berries and
bay leaves. Cover with cold brine and leave for three days before using.

Apple

1 Granny Smith apple
Cider vinegar pickling brine, cold

Cut the apple into quarters and remove the core. Slice the flesh very
thinly and cover with cold brine. These pickles will be ready in 30 minutes
and will keep for 24 hours only.

Zucchini

4 medium zucchini (aka courgettes), ends trimmed
1 teaspoon cumin seeds
4 bay leaves
White wine vinegar pickling brine, cold

On an angle, cut the zucchini into 3mm-thick slices and wash thoroughly.
Dry fry the cumin seeds in a non-stick frying pan over a medium heat for
a few minutes, until you can smell their spiciness. Keep an eye on them,
as they can easily burn. Place the zucchini, seeds and bay leaves in a Kilner
jar and cover with cold brine. Leave for at least 24 hours before using.

Carrot

6 medium carrots, peeled and trimmed
100g fresh root ginger
6 cardamom pods, lightly crushed
White wine vinegar pickling brine, hot

On an angle, cut the carrots into 3mm-thick slices and wash thoroughly.
Peel the ginger and cut into small chunks. Place the carrot, ginger and
cardamom into a Kilner jar and cover with hot brine. Leave for three
days before using.

Cauliflower

1 medium cauliflower
2 teaspoons coriander seeds
White wine vinegar pickling brine, hot

Remove and discard the leaves from the cauliflower and break off
individual florets. Cut any large ones in half. Dry fry the coriander seeds
in a non-stick frying pan over a medium heat for a few minutes, until
you can smell their spiciness. Keep an eye on them, as they can easily
burn. Place the florets and coriander seeds in a Kilner jar and cover
with hot brine. Leave for three days before using.

Celery

4 celery sticks, ends trimmed and strings peeled
1 teaspoon celery seeds
Cider vinegar pickling brine, cold

Cut the celery sticks on an angle into bite-sized slices and wash
thoroughly. Place in a Kilner jar with the celery seeds and cover
with cold brine. Leave for at least two days before using.

Pizzette

There are approximately two thousand pizza joints in New York City. This number doesn't include restaurants that happen to serve pizza as part of a broader menu. Pizza is a very big deal. There are even (otherwise sane) New Yorkers who will quite soberly inform you that pizza was invented in New York City at the end of the nineteenth century and that Lombardi's in Little Italy was the first full-blown, specialist pizza restaurant in America. This last part might be true – Lombardi's coal-fired pizza oven has been knocking out excellent rough-crust pizza since 1905 – but the rest seems a little far-fetched. The passionate *pizzaioli* of Naples and the San Marzano tomato growers on the slopes of Mount Vesuvius might beg to differ.

Still, much of the pizza in the Big Apple is undeniably excellent. Many of the pioneers of New York-style pizza (think Neapolitan-style but bigger) are still operating and are formally on the pizza tourist trail: John's of Bleecker Street, Lombardi's, Grimaldi's, Di Fara. At SPUNTINO we don't even attempt to emulate the pizzas of New York City, normally around the size of a truck's hubcap. Ours are diminutive pizzette: around 20cm or 8 inches in diameter and much more manageable as part of a small-plate feast.

As ever, the dough is not just the starting point but perhaps the most important element of a good pizza. There needs to be a degree of irregularity in terms of shape and thickness in order for the dough to form an outer edge that has bubbling, charring and crispness – known in Naples as the *cornicione*. Please don't fret if your pizzette are not perfectly round – they will taste all the better for their wonkiness.

Good pizza is also dependent on the oven being as hot as possible. Wood-fired professional ovens reach temperatures of 450°C and cook pizzas in a matter of 1–2 minutes. You won't be able to replicate that at home, but most domestic ovens, preheated to the max, can reach 240–250°C (Gas 9 or more), and you can help things along by using a pizza stone (or, less effective, a good baking sheet). With a little preparation, you should be able to nonchalantly pull off these crowd-pleasers to great effect.

Basic Pizza or Pizzetta Dough

There are few kitchen activities that give me as much pleasure as making bread. This is partly to do with the alchemic transformation of flour and water into loaves, buns or pizzas, and partly to do with the deeply therapeutic process of kneading dough. In fact, I have a confession: one of my favourite task-avoidance strategies, particularly when I should be writing, is baking bread. It is classic procrastination, but I figure that if it produces something worthwhile and tasty at the end of it, it can't be all that bad.

As well as being perfect for ten or so pizzetta bases, this bread dough makes a very decent loaf too; just prove the dough for a second time in a loaf tin before baking for 20 minutes.

For about ten pizzetta bases:
15g fresh yeast (or 1 x 7g sachet fast-action yeast)
300ml tepid water
500g strong white flour – Italian 00 is best – plus extra for dusting
15g (two teaspoons) fine salt
2 tablespoons extra virgin olive oil

With a whisk or a fork, vigorously combine the fresh yeast and the warm water, and set aside for 5 minutes. I like to see a little froth on the surface. (To make cold water tepid simply add a good splash from a boiled kettle, by the way.)

Mix the flour and the salt in a large mixing bowl with the olive oil and the yeasty water. (If using dried yeast, mix the flour, salt and yeast together in a large bowl, then add the water and olive oil.) Stir with a wooden spoon or get your hands dirty to form the mixture into a dough.

Once the dough has formed and is nicely sticky but still rolls into a ball, transfer to a lightly floured surface. Knead the dough by pushing it backwards and forwards simultaneously with your two hands so that you are stretching it and then bullying it back down into a ball. Repeat this, giving the dough a good working over. You shouldn't get too puffed out but it will be like a gym session for your hands and arms, and you will feel the dough becoming smooth and springy. After 10 minutes of kneading, push the dough back into a ball, flour the top, put back in the cleaned bowl, and cover with oiled clingfilm. Leave to rise in a warm place.

When the ball of dough has doubled in size, usually after about an hour, it is ready. Separate into ten even-sized pieces and then, on a very lightly floured surface, roll into rough, thin 20cm discs. Place on a work surface for 15 minutes to rest briefly, and then top with the rest of your ingredients and cook, following your chosen recipe. The easiest way to transfer your pizzette to the oven is on a pizza blade or 'peel'. But a couple of metal spatulas or fish slices will do.

If you want to use the dough later, place the small balls of dough on a tray, cover with a damp cloth or oiled clingfilm and leave in the fridge. They'll be good for up to 24 hours. Just remember to take them out half an hour before you want to use them.

Basic Tomato Sauce

A good tomato sauce is such a useful commodity to have to hand and, although the convenience of tinned passata has made shortcuts incredibly tempting, I would still recommend that you make a big batch of this sauce and save what you don't use in the fridge (where it will keep for up to a week) or freezer.

For 1.5 litres:
100ml extra virgin olive oil
1 onion, finely sliced
1 garlic clove, chopped
Scant ½ tablespoon fine salt
¾ teaspoon black pepper
Small pinch of chilli flakes
750g fresh tomatoes, quartered
3 x 400g tins of chopped tomatoes
Small handful of fresh oregano, chopped
Caster sugar, if necessary

Heat half the oil in a saucepan on a medium-low flame and in it sweat the onion, garlic, salt, pepper and chilli for 15 minutes. When the onions are glossy and transparent, add the fresh tomatoes and the rest of the oil and cook gently for a further 15 minutes.

Add the tinned tomatoes, bring to a gentle bubble and then simmer on a very low heat for 1 hour.

Take the pan off the heat and add the chopped oregano. You can season the sauce with a little sugar, to taste – it will depend on how sweet your tomatoes are. Transfer to a food blender or use a hand-blender to blitz for a few minutes. If you like, pass through a fine sieve.

Fennel Salami, Caper & Chilli Pizzetta

Fennel salami (or *finocchiona*) is one of my favourite sausages and one that is much celebrated in Tuscany, from where it comes. Dry-cured lean pork shoulder and fatty pork cheek, spiced with fennel, then aged for up to a year, are the secrets to this fantastically flavoursome *salame*. Cooking it makes it even tastier. I find the best capers for this pizzetta are the very dainty Sicilian variety.

For one pizzetta:
1 pizzetta base – see page 86
1 tablespoon Basic Tomato Sauce – see page 89 – or tomato passata
25g grated block mozzarella – the hard, cheap kind
4 slices of fennel salami (*finocchiona*)
1 tablespoon grated Parmesan
1 teaspoon capers
½ teaspoon chilli flakes

Preheat your oven on its highest setting. If you are using a pizza stone (which I highly recommend), allow 15 minutes for it to get really hot. (An alternative is a good metal baking sheet.) The temperature should be at least 240–250°C, which is Gas 9 or over, but get it higher if you can.

On to your pizzetta base, gently spoon a thin layer of tomato sauce (or passata), then sprinkle over the grated mozzarella. Place the slices of *finocchiona* on top. Scatter over the grated Parmesan, capers and chilli.

Cook on the pizza stone in your preheated oven for about 6–10 minutes (depending on how hot your oven can go) or until the edges start to bubble and burn.

Cauliflower & Scamorza Pizzetta

Scamorza is a cow's milk curd cheese, similar in appearance to mozzarella. It originates in Puglia where makers traditionally form it into a ball shape before 'strangling' it a third of the way down with a piece of string to give it the distinctive pear shape you will see at the delicatessen cheese counter. It has a much stronger taste than mozzarella and melts particularly well on pizzas.

For one pizzetta:
1 pizzetta base – see page 86
Fine salt
¼ small cauliflower, broken into florets
Extra virgin olive oil
Small handful of sage leaves, roughly chopped
1 garlic clove, finely chopped
Flaky sea salt and black pepper
2 shallots, quartered
60g grated Scamorza
30g Gorgonzola

Preheat the oven to 180°C/Gas 4.

Place a pan of salted water over a high heat and bring to the boil, then add the cauliflower florets and cook for a few minutes until just tender. Drain, pat dry, slice and place on a baking tray. Drizzle with olive oil to coat and mix in the sage and half the garlic. Season generously with salt and pepper and bake in the preheated oven for 5–8 minutes. Remove from the oven and set aside to cool.

Meanwhile, place the shallots in a small heavy-based pan. Add a glug of olive oil, the remainder of the garlic and season well with salt and pepper. Place over the lowest heat and cover with a lid. Every minute or so, stir the shallots so that they don't stick to the bottom of the pan. Continue cooking until they are completely soft and translucent, about 8 minutes. Set aside.

Now, turn the oven up to its highest setting (240-250°C/Gas 9 or above). At the same time put a pizza stone or baking sheet in the oven to heat up.

Sprinkle the grated Scamorza evenly over the pizzetta base, then scatter over the cooled cauliflower slices. Spoon over the cooked shallots and finally crumble on the Gorgonzola.

Cook on the pizza stone in your preheated oven for about 6-10 minutes (depending on how hot your oven can go) or until the edges start to bubble.

Potato, Anchovy & Nettle Pizzetta

Yes, stinging nettles, burning maple, burn weed, *Urtica dioica*. It's a horrible plant if your bare legs or arms brush against it on a woodland walk, but soaked in water and cooked, the toxins wash away, leaving behind a surprisingly benign leaf, high in vitamins A and C, iron, calcium, potassium and manganese, and packed with protein too. Peak season for stinging nettles is spring, when you will find them absolutely everywhere. Remember to take some gloves and a bag with you next time you go for a walk in the woods, and make sure you pick the nice bright green leaves, not the manky old ones.

For one pizzetta:
1 pizzetta base - see page 86
Fine salt
200g wild nettles, leaves picked and washed
1 teaspoon Dijon mustard
2 garlic cloves, finely chopped
1 tablespoon grated Parmesan
Flaky sea salt and black pepper
100ml extra virgin olive oil
2 small new potatoes
40g grated block mozzarella - the hard, cheap kind
7 brown anchovies, from a tin

Place a pan of salted water over a high heat. Once it has come to the boil, blanch the nettles for 2 minutes, then drain and squeeze out any excess liquid, as you might with cooked spinach. This removes the toxins. Place the cooked nettle leaves in a food processor with the mustard, chopped garlic, Parmesan, a good pinch of salt and pepper and blend. With the motor still running, add the olive oil.

Slice the potatoes very thinly and wash them really well to remove the sticky starch. Bring a pan of salted water to the boil and add the sliced potatoes, cooking vigorously for 2 minutes. Gently drain and lay out on a clean kitchen cloth to dry them.

Preheat your oven to the max (240-250°C/Gas 9 or above). At the same time put a pizza stone or baking sheet in the oven to heat up. Scatter the grated mozzarella over the pizzetta base and arrange the cooked potato over the top, seasoning with a pinch each of salt and pepper. Spoon over a good few dollops of the cooked nettles and then drape the anchovies over the top.

Cook on the pizza stone in your preheated oven for about 6-10 minutes (depending on how hot your oven can go) or until the edges start to burn.

Fig, Coppa & Gorgonzola Pizzetta

Coppa is a versatile cured ham from the neck and shoulder of the pig and is traditionally found in the region at the top left of Emilia-Romagna, just north of Parma. It is dry-salted rather than brined and sometimes the skin is rubbed with hot paprika before being hung and cured. It's my favourite *salume*.

Make sure you buy ripe figs – unlike other fruits, figs do not ripen once picked. You can wait forever – but they'll rot first.

For one pizzetta:
1 pizzetta base – see page 86
20g grated block mozzarella – the hard, cheap kind
4 slices of coppa
2 ripe figs, washed, top and bottom trimmed off
40g Dolcelatte (Gorgonzola Dolce)
1 teaspoon flaky sea salt
½ teaspoon black pepper

Preheat your oven to its highest setting (240-250°C/Gas 9 or above). At the same time put a pizza stone or baking sheet in the oven to heat up.

Scatter the grated mozzarella evenly over the pizzetta base, then arrange the coppa on top. Slice the figs into thick discs and then place them over the coppa. Break the Dolcelatte up into small chunks and drop them evenly around the pizzetta. Season with the salt and pepper.

Cook on the pizza stone in your preheated oven for about 6-10 minutes (depending on how hot your oven can go) or until you see some charring or bubbling around the edges.

Wild Mushroom & Taleggio Pizzetta

'Wild mushrooms' cover a multitude of seasonal possibilities. Porcini or penny buns appear in the markets through autumn and winter, transforming menus everywhere. Field and oyster mushrooms are reliable standbys, but I get truly excited when I come across beefsteaks, or ox tongues. These bracket fungi have an acidic flavour that requires a little skill in the cooking, but they are terrifyingly flesh-like, with a marvellous texture. In spring and summer I look forward to my favourites, morels and chanterelles – both beautifully subtle but with the ability to lift any dish, and brilliant in risotto.

But if you can't get hold of good wild fungi, don't panic. Portobello or chestnut mushrooms from the supermarket will do just fine.

For one pizzetta:
1 pizzetta base – see page 86
50g mixed wild mushrooms
Extra virgin olive oil
Flaky sea salt and black pepper
1 garlic clove, finely chopped
30g grated block mozzarella – the hard, cheap kind
40g Taleggio, cut into 5 pieces
3 sprigs of oregano, leaves picked and roughly chopped

Preheat the oven to the max (240-250°C/Gas 9 or above). At the same time put a pizza stone or baking sheet in the oven to heat up.

Pick through the mushrooms, brushing off any dust, and slice them into even pieces. Place a frying pan over a high heat and add a glug of the olive oil. Once hot, quickly sauté the mushrooms, a couple of minutes, then season with salt, pepper and garlic. Set aside.

Scatter the grated mozzarella evenly over the pizzetta base. Distribute the cooked mushrooms evenly over this and then arrange the pieces of Taleggio on top. Sprinkle with the chopped oregano.

Cook on the pizza stone in your preheated oven for about 6-10 minutes (depending on how hot your oven can go) or until the dough starts to blister.

Fennel, Chilli & Caperberry Pizzetta

This is a lovely, fragrant pizzetta with a real emphasis on summer and freshness.

The chilli, by the way, should be a reasonably hot variety as it lifts the whole show a little higher. I am not a fan of the lazy bottles of chilli oil you often find in high-street pizza restaurants – there is really no substitute for freshly chopped chilli peppers.

For one pizzetta:
1 pizzetta base - see page 86
1 fennel bulb, washed and thinly sliced
1 long red chilli, deseeded and finely chopped
1 garlic clove, finely chopped
Flaky sea salt and black pepper
Extra virgin olive oil
Grated zest of 1 lemon
30g grated block mozzarella - the hard, cheap kind
Small handful of caperberries
1 tablespoon grated Parmesan

Preheat the oven to its highest setting (240-250°C/Gas 9 or above). At the same time put a pizza stone or baking sheet in the oven to heat up.

Put the fennel, chilli, garlic, a good pinch each of salt and pepper, 4 tablespoons olive oil and the lemon zest into a bowl and leave to marinate for 20 minutes.

Scatter the grated mozzarella evenly over the pizzetta base. Distribute the marinated fennel evenly over the cheese, and top with the caperberries and grated Parmesan.

Cook on the pizza stone in your preheated oven for about 6-10 minutes (depending on how hot your oven can go) or until the dough starts to char. Finally, before serving, sprinkle with a flourish of olive oil.

Cicoria & Fontina Pizzetta

London suffers from a paucity of street markets and a limited range of readily available bitter leaves, salads, chicories and brassicas. In Italy it is a different story; I am frequently bamboozled by the abundance of produce. So it is always a delight when one of our grocer suppliers brings in something out-of-the-ordinary, usually in very short season. Quite often our chefs will call me when taking delivery of Castelfranco or tardivo and I will make my way to Rupert Street as quickly as I can. Cicoria is one such treat and its bitterness is a lovely foil to Fontina's soft sweetness.

If you struggle to find cicoria, chard makes a respectable substitute.

For one pizzetta:
1 pizzetta base - see page 86
Fine salt
¼ head of cicoria (or 2-3 stalks of Swiss chard)
1 garlic clove, finely chopped
Extra virgin olive oil
Flaky sea salt and black pepper
50g grated Fontina

Preheat the oven to its highest setting (240-250°C/Gas 9 or above). At the same time put a pizza stone or baking sheet in the oven to heat up.

Place a pan of salted water over a high heat. Meanwhile cut the base off the cicoria and discard. Cut the stalks on an angle into bite-sized pieces. Separate the stalky bits from the leafier pieces. Once the water has come up to the boil drop the stalks in and cook for a minute then drop the leaves in and boil for a further 20 seconds. Drain immediately, and when cool enough to handle, squeeze out excess water. Set aside.

Gently heat the garlic in a frying pan with a glug of olive oil, then dress the hot cicoria with the oily garlic, and some flaky salt and black pepper. Set aside.

Scatter the Fontina evenly over the pizzetta base and distribute the cicoria over the top. Cook on the pizza stone in your preheated oven for about 6-10 minutes (depending on how hot your oven can go) or until the crust starts to bubble.

Cavolo Nero, Fig & Olive Pizzetta

There are so many delicious varieties of olive, with subtle flavour differences, colours and textures, that the disappointing grey and plasticky pizza-restaurant standard just doesn't pass muster. We use Kalamata, with their deep salinity and a lovely purple hue, which have the added bonus of being easy to get hold of.

For one pizzetta:
1 pizzetta base – see page 86
1–2 dried figs, stemmed and quartered
4 Kalamata olives, pitted
½ tablespoon oregano leaves
½ garlic clove, peeled
½ tablespoon sherry vinegar
Flaky sea salt and black pepper
Extra virgin olive oil
4 small or 2 large cavolo nero leaves, stalks removed and discarded
40g grated block mozzarella – the hard, cheap kind

Put the figs into a saucepan and cover them with water. Place the pan over a medium heat, bring to the boil, then turn down and simmer for about 20 minutes. Drain the figs and place them in the small bowl of a food processor with the olives, oregano, garlic, vinegar and a pinch each of salt and pepper. Start processing – you may need to scrape the mixture down the sides – and then slowly add 1 tablespoon of olive oil, turning the mixture into a dark sludge.

Place another pan of salted water over a high heat. Cut the cavolo nero leaves into 3cm pieces. Once the water is bubbling, quickly blanch the leaves for about 30 seconds. Drain and, when cool enough to handle, squeeze out any excess water. Season lightly with sea salt, black pepper and a drizzle of extra virgin olive oil.

Preheat the oven to its highest setting (240–250°C/Gas 9 or above). At the same time put a pizza stone or baking sheet in the oven to heat up.

Scatter the mozzarella over the pizzetta base, then arrange the cavolo nero over this. Distribute several dollops of the fig and olive mix on top of the cavolo nero.

Cook on the pizza stone in your preheated oven for about 6–10 minutes (depending on how hot your oven can go) or until the crust just starts to burn nicely.

New-season Garlic & Goat Curd Pizzetta

Here's a very tasty pizzetta that makes use of the lovely green and purple new-season garlic, available every year from April/May. It's plump and waxy and significantly milder in flavour than the dried white bulbs we see throughout the rest of the year. By pre-baking the cloves you produce a delicately flavoured paste that works beautifully with the goat curd and green olives.

New-season garlic always appears at farmers' markets in the spring, occasionally in good supermarkets, or you could ask your greengrocer to get some for you.

For one pizzetta:
1 pizzetta base – see page 86
1 head of new-season garlic, skin on
Extra virgin olive oil
2 tablespoons pitted green olives
A few sprigs of oregano, leaves picked and finely chopped
Juice of ½ lemon
Flaky sea salt and black pepper
50g grated block mozzarella – the hard, cheap kind
100g goat curd

Preheat the oven to 160°C/Gas 3. Separate the cloves of the garlic and place them on a baking tray. Drizzle a little olive oil over the cloves and cover well with foil. Place in the preheated oven and cook for about 30-40 minutes. The garlic is ready when it is really soft, and you can squeeze it out like toothpaste.

Meanwhile finely chop the green olives and place them in a bowl with the chopped oregano, lemon juice, a large pinch of sea salt and a large twist of black pepper. Mix well and set aside.

Once the garlic is cooked, remove it from the oven. Turn the oven up to its highest setting (240-250°C/Gas 9 or above). At the same time put a pizza stone or baking sheet in the oven to heat up.

Squeeze the garlic paste from the cloves evenly over the pizzetta base. Scatter with the grated mozzarella and evenly distribute dollops of the green olive mix.

Cook on the pizza stone in the preheated oven for about 6-10 minutes (depending on how hot your oven can go) or until the edges are blistering. Once cooked, spoon over the goat curd, and drizzle with some extra virgin olive oil.

Purple-sprouting Broccoli & Spicy Sausage Pizzetta

Spicy sausage with broccoli is such a winning combination that I often mix them together with fusilli pasta twists as an easy supper for my children. Here on a pizzetta it is better to use the small, long florets of sprouting broccoli, and it's worth sourcing very good spicy sausages from a delicatessen.

For one pizzetta:
1 pizzetta base – see page 86
2 small spicy Italian sausages
Extra virgin olive oil
85g purple-sprouting broccoli
1 garlic clove, finely chopped
¼ teaspoon chilli flakes
Flaky sea salt and black pepper
50g grated block mozzarella – the hard, cheap kind
1 tablespoon grated Parmesan

Preheat the oven to 180°C/Gas 4. Don't prick the sausages (that's right), place them in a roasting tin, coat them with a little olive oil and give them a shake. Cook in the preheated oven for 15 minutes. Remove and allow them to cool.

Place a saucepan of salted water over a high heat. Meanwhile trim the root ends of the broccoli; cut in smaller pieces if long. Once the water is boiling, cook the broccoli until just tender – about 6 minutes – and drain well. Gently soften the garlic in a frying pan with a glug of olive oil. Dress the broccoli with the garlic and oil, chilli flakes, a pinch of sea salt and a little black pepper. Keep to one side.

Turn the oven up to full whack (240-250°C/Gas 9 or above). At the same time put a pizza stone or baking sheet in the oven to heat up.

The sausages will be cool enough to handle now, so slice them into bite-sized pieces. Scatter the mozzarella over the pizzetta base, then distribute the broccoli and chopped sausage on top. Sprinkle with the Parmesan.

Cook on the pizza stone in your preheated oven for 6-10 minutes (depending on how hot your oven can go) or until the edges are starting to blister.

Cime di Rapa & Smoked Ricotta Pizzetta

Smoked ricotta is a bit of a revelation, a refreshing alternative to the usual mozzarella, fluffier and with hickory notes. But here the cime di rapa is the star. It's one of those ingredients that sounds wrong on paper – the English translation is 'turnip tops'. These are the leaves that grow out of the root – but they are as special as any bitter leaves I know.

For one pizzetta:
1 pizzetta base - see page 86
Fine salt
250g cime di rapa
1 garlic clove, finely chopped
Extra virgin olive oil
Flaky sea salt and black pepper
2 tablespoons Basic Tomato Sauce - see page 89 - or tomato passata
50g smoked ricotta

Place a medium pan of water over a high heat and add a pinch of fine salt. While the water heats, prepare the cime di rapa. Trim the thick base and discard, separate the stalks from the leaves and cut both into bite-sized pieces. Once the water has come up to the boil, add the stalks and blanch for a minute. Then add the leaves and cook for another 20 seconds. Drain and, when cool enough to handle, squeeze out excess liquid.

Preheat the oven to its highest setting (240-250°C/Gas 9 or above). At the same time put a pizza stone or baking sheet in the oven to heat up.

Gently soften the garlic in a frying pan with a glug of olive oil and then dress the hot cime di rapa along with a pinch each of flaky sea salt and black pepper.

Smear the pizzetta base with the tomato sauce/passata, making sure you take it out to the edges. Scatter over the cooked cime di rapa and then crumble the smoked ricotta on top.

Cook on the pizza stone in the preheated oven for about 6-10 minutes (depending on how hot your oven can go) or until the edges are blistering.

Milano's

Joe's Dairy

Little Italy, NoLIta, SoHo

About 2 miles
45 minutes walking plus pit stops
Best time of day: 11am
Subway: Broadway-Lafayette Street, F, D, M and B trains; or Bleecker Street, 6 train

Warning: Opening times change and places come and go. Please check availability before heading to any specific eating place.

From the subway, walk a couple of blocks east along Houston, past Mulberry Street, to take a peek at two venerable and gorgeously scruffy New York institutions that sit almost next to each other. Milano's (51 E. Houston St) is a grungy dive bar with a genuine layer of dust over just about everything. Jackie, who has been tending the bar for decades, will point out the eccentric and gloriously decrepit interiors while you stay to indulge in a late-morning beer or seltzer. Emilio's Ballato (55 E. Houston St) has the scars and lines of age that can't be faked. It has genuine rock'n'roll credentials, too: the walls are covered with photographs and personal messages from the likes of David Bowie, Billy Joel, Lionel Richie and Rihanna. If you are there early you might get to see the restaurant being set up or be lucky enough to catch Emilio for a chat.

Head west for a busy walk along Houston to Sullivan Street, turning left where you will find the Shrine Church of Saint Anthony of Padua. There's a curious notice outside this rather austere edifice, that announces:

SICK CALLS – ANY TIME
BAPTISMS – BY APPOINTMENT
CONFESSIONS – SATURDAY 4PM TO 5PM

It has always struck me that either the local congregation is remarkably sin-free, or confession is a particularly efficient process.

Nearby, there are a couple of lovely shopfronts that are worth looking at. Firstly there is Joe's Dairy (156 Sullivan St) just opposite the church. It was a thriving business until only a few years ago, selling excellent mozzarella with charm and good humour. But last year I noticed it had closed. Sad days. The shopfront remains intact and I love the bold, no-nonsense lettering in red and green. I wonder how much longer it will be there.

Joe's Dairy

Emilio's Ballato

On the other side and further down the street, Once Upon a Tart (135 Sullivan St) is a modern cake shop and café with a beautiful quadruple timber frontage. And then, the next corner on the left as you head south, you turn onto Prince Street. Between Thompson and West Broadway you will come across the truly gorgeous storefront of what used to be Vesuvio Bakery (160 Prince St). The frontage and interior remain the same but it now operates as the Birdbath Bakery. It's worth your while pausing for a homemade oatmeal and raisin cookie or their famous chocolate chip variety – you've got some walking ahead of you.

A ten-minute walk east along Prince Street will take you through SoHo back to the tiny neighbourhood of NoLIta (North of Little Italy). On Elizabeth Street between Prince and Houston you will find two more delightful shopfronts.

Albanese Meats & Poultry (238 Elizabeth St) is a fantastic blast from the past: an old-school butcher shop run by Moe Albanese who was born in 1923. Mr Albanese still cuts meat on a tatty wooden block and proudly shows off his wares to anyone who asks. The storefront is painted fire-engine red and in the left-hand window there's an immense set of scales with the words 'Thank You – Call Again', while in the right window there is a sign saying HOME OF THE 'I GOT'CHA' STEAKS. I have no idea what 'I got'cha' steaks might be, but one day I must pop in and ask Mr Albanese.

On the opposite side of Elizabeth Street at number 237 is an old shopfront that has been preserved despite the shop having shut down years ago. It is now a gallery or boutique or some-such, but the fascia proudly announces 'Moe's Meat Market' in garish green and red. Inside the white wipe-down walls still remain; another lovely echo from a New York that is slowly vanishing.

Now head back south on Elizabeth for three blocks, and then turn right onto Broome Street. Two more blocks west brings you to Mulberry Street. Look up and you will see two immense signs; one steel and neon monster advertising GROTTA AZZURRA and a second, as you turn left into

Once Upon a Tart

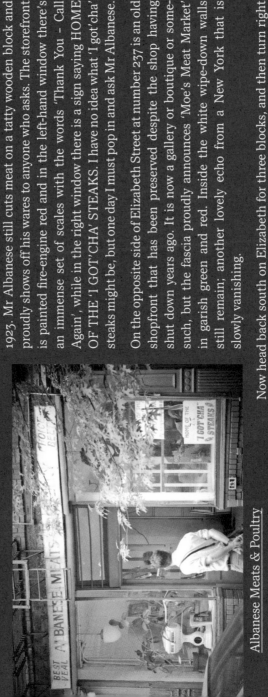

Albanese Meats & Poultry

Little Italy, NoLIta, SoHo

Mulberry Street, announcing the start of Little Italy. Just on your left as you stroll south you will see the Mulberry Street Bar (176 Mulberry St). This joint featured in more than one episode of the seminal gangster series *The Sopranos* and a pivotal scene in *Donnie Brasco*. The window proudly displays photos of famous customers – Al Pacino, James Gandolfini, Ronald Reagan – and I especially like the faded copper panels on the doors recording decades of rough-and-tumble. It's worth lingering for a cold beer or refreshing lemonade at the bar.

Mulberry Street Bar

As you continue south you will be struck by the sheer number of Italian restaurants, all jostling for position as Little Italy's best, oldest, most famous or most authentic. Their signs and shopfronts try to outdo each other with Italian flags, pictures of 'Nonna', celebrity endorsements, comedy Mafia associations, dates of origin, basket-weave Chianti bottles, plastic grape vines and chequered tablecloths. These restaurants are what New Yorkers affectionately call 'red sauce joints' and while they have a certain charm, there is a whiff of the theme park about them. If it's lunchtime and you're hungry, you could do worse than head to Umberto's Clam House (132 Mulberry St, between Grand and Hester). As well as a fine plate of linguine vongole, you will be able to soak up the genuine Mafia connections of this humble spaghetti house. In 1972, just two months after the restaurant opened, a notorious mobster named Joe Gallo was murdered here by two gunmen from a rival gang while dining with his family and bodyguard.

Retrace your steps north along Mulberry until you reach the junction with Grand Street. On one corner you will see the rather lovely Italian Food Center (186 Grand St) with its evocative signage and neat red-brick frontage; on the other you will see Alleva (188 Grand St), one of the oldest and most evocative delicatessens in downtown Manhattan.

Piemonte Ravioli Co.

Italian Food Center

E Rossi & Co

Di Palo's

Alleva was established in 1892, an historical fact announced by an elaborate crest at the back of the shop above the cheese display. I love the aluminium shopfront, the green and white floor tiles, the F. ALLEVA mosaic on the front step, the window signs that shout MOZZARELLA and RICOTTA, and the morning's bread stacked on a display rack facing the street. In contrast to the Disneyland feel of the touristy restaurants, here is a place that is a living, breathing part of the city: a place used by many hundreds of New Yorkers on a daily basis and gloriously patinated because of it.

Next door you will see the Piemonte Ravioli Co (190 Grand St), established 1920, with its window display of improbably coloured pasta. Across the way is E Rossi & Co (193 Grand St), an ancient store, packed with religious artefacts and specialising, it seems, in nativity scenes. Alongside is the Ferrara Gelato Bar (195 Grand St), established 1892, purveyors of ice cream to the city twenty-four hours a day. You can't miss it – the shopfront sign dwarfs everything around. If you feel the need for a sweet fix, this is the place to indulge in a couple of scoops of mint-choc-chip with hot fudge sauce.

Across the road now to the final treat. Di Palo's (200 Grand St) is one of the busiest delis in Manhattan, characterised by the scores of hanging meats and regiments of white-coated shop assistants. It feels more like a market than a shop, and is certain to make you salivate. My advice is to pick up some non-perishable souvenirs – olive oil, marinated artichokes, dried pasta, panforte. If you engage with one of the deli assistants, you might even be able to enjoy an impromptu olive oil tasting. This may sound cynical, but I have never known this little demonstration not to result in a sale.

Alleva

Ferrara Gelato Bar

Salads & Dressings

As a restaurateur who still occasionally likes to put on an apron and take an order, I have noticed that it is a peculiarly American (and particularly Californian) trait to order salads without dressing, or with it on the side.

In my opinion, a salad is not a salad until it is dressed. It is the dressing that pulls the ingredients together. It is the dressing that announces the flavours. It is the dressing that creates a dish that is greater than the sum of its individual parts.

At SPUNTINO, the salads are not just something that goes with something else. For a restaurant that is known for its hearty food, it may seem incongruous to offer such a large selection of greens, leaves, pulses and beans, but they often upstage the more obvious showstoppers. And while we all get very excited at the freshness and newness of first-of-the-season English asparagus, Treviso tardivo, Castelfranco or Kent cobnuts, I am also a big fan of cooked salads. This may sound oxymoronic, but warm ingredients work surprisingly well in salads; the flavour-enhancing qualities of heat can frequently improve a leafy ensemble.

Some of these recipes specify the use of a mandoline. It is a relatively inexpensive kitchen gadget and one that allows you to slice raw ingredients remarkably thinly – I do recommend you invest in a decent model to make your salad-making life a lot easier. If you don't have a mandoline, however, just make sure you have a very sharp knife or a French – or swivel-headed – peeler to get those wafer-thin results.

Finally, a word on tossing. What the 'dressing-on-the-side' brigade seems not to realise is that just pouring oil and vinegar over a salad doesn't count as dressing it at all. You need to use a large mixing bowl to prepare your salads (I have a very deep stainless-steel one at home for this very purpose) and you need to use your hands. Gently turn your ingredients, softly moving them around the bowl, taking care not to crush, crease or bruise. I put some of the dressing in the bowl first – it helps to accelerate the mixing and is less damaging to the ingredients. Don't over-dress – the leaves should only just be coated. Your salads will taste so much brighter if you treat them in this delicate, courteous and respectful way.

Chopped Salad

There are certain things I can never resist when I see them
on a restaurant menu. Anything with a soft-poached egg.
Anything with bone marrow. Burrata. And I can never stop
myself ordering a chopped salad.

What distinguishes chopped salads from their fuller-
bodied counterparts is the ease with which the ingredients
combine. The act of dicing the constituent parts somehow
elevates them and gives the ensemble a little more finesse.

I am especially fond of the tarragon dressing used for
this salad and I often use it elsewhere when I want a fragrant,
slightly aniseedy alternative to vinaigrette. (Incidentally, did
you know that the Italian word for the herb is *dragoncello*?
How lovely is that?)

For four:
1 baby gem lettuce
1 yellow chicory
1 red chicory
½ cucumber, peeled, deseeded and diced
4 celery sticks, peeled and diced
½ bunch of spring onions, sliced thinly on an angle
Small handful of tarragon leaves, chopped
4 tablespoons Tarragon Dressing – see page 149

Cut the baby gem in half lengthways, and then slice across into 1cm
pieces. Wash in iced water (in a bowl of water with some ice cubes) and
then place into a salad spinner. Cut the chicory in half lengthways. With
the tip of your knife, remove the core and discard. Now slice the chicory
in the same way as the gem, wash in cold water, and add to the spinner.

When the gem and chicory are washed and spun-dried, mix together
in a large bowl with the other ingredients. Add the dressing and coat
everything thoroughly.

Beetroot, Pistachio & Ricotta Salata Salad

There is such a world of difference between ricotta and ricotta salata that they almost deserve to be given different names. Both are made from whey, the by-product of cheese making, but the former is a curd, soft, creamy and white, while the latter is pressed, salted, dried, then aged.

There is a lovely contrast between the profound red of the beetroot and the pristine milky white of the ricotta salata; when plating, take care not to stain the cheese with the beets.

For six:
500g small beetroots, trimmed
1 teaspoon fine salt
2 teaspoons caster sugar
Red wine vinegar
100g pistachio nuts
2 shallots
1 bunch of watercress, washed
6 tablespoons Sherry Vinegar Dressing – see page 150
Flaky sea salt and black pepper
250g ricotta salata

First, wash the beetroots really well. Place them in a saucepan, cover with water and add the fine salt, the sugar and a good splash of red wine vinegar. Bring to the boil and reduce the heat to medium. Keep an eye on the water level – you may need to top it up to keep the beetroots covered. Cook for about 45 minutes to an hour, depending on the size of the beetroots. The best way to test whether a beetroot is done is to poke it with a sharp knife; if there is no give, it is ready.

Meanwhile, toast the pistachio nuts. Put them in a non-stick pan and dry fry over a medium heat until golden, a few minutes only. Leave to cool.

Once the beetroots are cooked, remove them from the heat and drain. While they are still warm, peel them. Unless you want to look like you have blood on your hands, I would recommend using kitchen gloves. When they are peeled, cut them into quarters, and place in a bowl. Thinly slice the shallots, add to the beetroot along with the watercress, and dress well with the dressing.

Once you have turned the beets over a few times with the dressing and the leaves, add a pinch of sea salt and a twist of black pepper. Transfer to a serving bowl or large plate, and crumble over the ricotta. Sprinkle the pistachio nuts on top, and serve.

Duck Ham, Pecorino & Mint Salad

Before you read any further, you need to know that you should start planning this dish eight days in advance, as you need to cure the raw duck breasts to turn them into mini 'hams'. But the results are, I promise, worth it.

Please put some thought into how to suspend the individual duck breasts – if you have one of those steel wire rack attachments in your fridge, it will be ideal. You will also need some muslin cloth and butcher's string. And when you come to assemble the salad, use a really sharp knife so that the slices of 'ham' are as thin as possible.

For six:
100g coarse sea salt
½ tablespoon black peppercorns
Small handful of thyme leaves
Grated zest of ½ orange
1 garlic clove
2 duck breasts, skin on

For the salad:
100g lamb's leaf lettuce
85g pea shoots, picked and washed
Small handful of mint leaves, sliced
1 bunch of spring onions, thinly sliced on an angle
6 tablespoons Vinaigrette - see page 147
50g Pecorino
Small handful of garlic chives (optional)

Place the sea salt, peppercorns, thyme, orange zest and garlic in a food processor and blend. (You could use a mortar and pestle.) Sprinkle half this salt mix into a clean plastic container and arrange the duck breasts neatly on top, then cover with the rest of the salt mix. Cover well and refrigerate for 24 hours.

The next day wash the duck breasts thoroughly and pat them dry. Wrap each one completely in muslin cloth and, using butcher's string, truss each of the breasts making sure you leave enough string to be able to hang them and still tie a sturdy knot. Suspend in the refrigerator, free from any contact or obstruction, and leave for seven days.

After they have spent a week curing in your fridge, remove the breasts and, using that super-sharp knife, slice the duck as thinly as you can. Once they are sliced, you can cut off the layer of fat if you wish.

Meanwhile place the lamb's leaf, pea shoots, mint and spring onions in a large mixing bowl and coat with the dressing. Gently turn a few times with your hand. Add the slices of duck ham and turn again before dividing equally onto six plates. Finally, shave the Pecorino over the salads, scatter over the garlic chives, if using, and serve.

Romaine, Soft-boiled Egg & Salt Cod Salad

This salad requires two days' advance preparation. The dressing is a main character here, not a supporting player, and uses one of my favourite ingredients, salt cod. It dramatically elevates the Romaine lettuce and the soft-boiled egg.

You will find salt cod in Spanish and Italian delicatessens where it is normally wrapped in cellophane, hard and flat. Salt is a great preservative, of course, but you have to remove the majority of it and that process takes a little time. After two days of soaking and rinsing, the flesh starts to flake away from the bones and is ready to use. This soaking/rinsing process is also involved in making the Venetian classic *baccalà mantecato*.

For six:
½ loaf day-old bread, around 300g
Extra virgin olive oil
2 garlic cloves, crushed
6 medium eggs
1 large Romaine lettuce, smaller leaves left whole, larger ones sliced, washed and dried
2 shallots, thinly sliced
Flaky sea salt and black pepper

For the dressing:
200g salt cod fillet
1 litre milk
2 bay leaves
Sprig of rosemary
4 black peppercorns
½ head of garlic, cut in half horizontally
Strip of lemon peel
1 medium egg yolk
1 teaspoon Dijon mustard
2 tablespoons white wine vinegar
1 teaspoon lemon juice
100ml vegetable oil

Wash the salt cod in cold water and soak in a cool place (or the fridge) for 24 hours. Wash again and soak in fresh water for another 24 hours. Remove from the water and rinse well.

Place the salt cod in a pan and cover with the milk. Add the bay leaves, rosemary, peppercorns, garlic and lemon peel. Place a small plate on top of the cod within the pan to keep it completely submerged. Put the pan on a high heat and, the moment it comes to the boil, reduce the heat

then simmer for about 20 minutes. Once cooked, gently lift the cod out of the pan and onto a tray. While it is still hot, remove the skin and bones and throw them away. Pass the cooking liquid through a fine strainer and reserve about 100ml of it.

Place the salt cod, egg yolk, mustard, vinegar and lemon juice in a food processor with a good pinch of salt and pepper. Once thoroughly combined, while the machine is running slowly, add the vegetable oil in a steady stream, and finally the reserved cooking liquid.

Preheat the oven to 180°C/Gas 4. Tear the bread into bite-sized chunks and put them into a bowl with a good glug of olive oil, a pinch of salt and the crushed garlic. Massage the oil into the bread, place on a baking tray and cook in the preheated oven for 10–12 minutes. Remove and allow to cool.

Bring a pan of water to the boil, add the eggs and boil for 6½ minutes then transfer to iced water (a bowl of water with ice cubes). Once the eggs have cooled down, gently peel them and set aside.

Place the lettuce, shallot slices and most of the croutons in a bowl. Coat well with the salt cod dressing and transfer to a serving plate, then scatter over the reserved croutons. Cut the eggs in half and arrange on top. Lightly season the eggs, and drizzle with a little extra virgin olive oil.

Tuscan Bread Salad

In Mediterranean countries tomatoes grow in such abundance that there are often surpluses, which either get pulped for sauces or go to waste. (The Spanish town of Buñol, near Valencia, every August hosts La Tomatina, a tomato-themed food fight attended by up to fifty thousand people. That's one way to get rid of your extra tomatoes, I suppose.) But for centuries in Italy – more specifically, Tuscany – the rural staple *panzanella* has combined ripe tomatoes with stale or day-old bread to great effect. This peasant dish has noble aspirations, and I could happily eat it all summer long. Use only ripe tomatoes, and make sure they are the best quality you can find.

For four:
About 500g day-old sourdough bread
Extra virgin olive oil
Flaky sea salt
1 garlic clove, crushed
1kg tomatoes in different colours (ideally heritage or heirloom varieties)
8 sprigs of thyme, leaves picked and chopped
6 tablespoons Sherry Vinegar Dressing – see page 150
1 bunch of basil, leaves picked

Preheat the oven to 180°C/Gas 4. Tear the bread into bite-sized chunks and put them into a large bowl with a good few glugs of olive oil, a large pinch of salt and the crushed garlic. Massage the oil into the bread, lay it out on a baking tray and cook in the preheated oven for 10–12 minutes. Remove and allow to cool.

Now, cut the tomatoes into quarters or halves so that the pieces are bite-sized, and place them into a large bowl with the chopped thyme. Add the cooled croutons to the tomatoes and generously dress with the dressing, using your hands to make sure the ingredients are fully coated. Leave everything to marinate for half an hour.

Tear the basil leaves and mix through the tomatoes. Serve immediately.

'Slaw

Never underestimate a good 'slaw. There is something
very comforting and satisfying about the crunch and the
tang you get with the best versions, and 'slaws are remarkably
successful as accompaniments to strong-flavoured meats and
barbecues. The etymology here is interesting: the word
'coleslaw' comes from the Dutch *coolsla*, meaning 'cabbage
salad'. These days, you can make 'slaw with any shreddable
vegetable but, call me old-fashioned, the SPUNTINO version
still has a cabbage, albeit a bitter Italian one, at its heart.

For six:
¼ medium celeriac, about 200g
1 medium zucchini (aka courgette)
½ red onion
1 fennel bulb, halved and cored
1 head of radicchio
¼ white cabbage, about 200g
Small handful of mint leaves, finely chopped
4-6 tablespoons Lemon Mustard Dressing - see page 146

Peel the celeriac and, using a mandoline or a very sharp knife, slice very
thinly. Take the thin slices and cut again to create very thin matchsticks.
Do the same with the zucchini, onion and fennel. Place in a large bowl.

Cut the radicchio in half vertically and remove the core. Using a large
sharp knife, shred the radicchio. Do the same with the white cabbage.

Add the radicchio, cabbage and mint to the bowl and coat everything
well with the dressing. Check the seasoning before serving.

Blood Orange, Walnut & Ricotta Salata Salad

A simple, bold combination of flavours. Blood oranges have a very short season, from January to March, and I always try to make the most of them. Blood orange juice also goes particularly well with a little vodka to make a spectacularly good Screwdriver.

For four:
2 blood oranges
50g walnut pieces
Large handful of watercress, washed
½ red onion, thinly sliced
4 tablespoons Walnut Dressing – see page 150
50g ricotta salata

Using a sharp knife remove the skin and pith from the blood oranges, and then segment them. Squeeze the denuded oranges to garner all of their juice. Remove any seeds.

Toast the walnut pieces by putting in a non-stick frying pan and dry frying over a medium heat until golden, a few minutes only. Cool, and then crush into smaller pieces, using a rolling pin.

Place the watercress and red onion in a bowl and add the dressing. Transfer to a serving plate and arrange the blood orange segments on top. Gently crumble the ricotta salata into pieces and scatter over the top along with the crushed walnuts.

Pink Fir, Chicory & Dill Salad

Here's a nice plate of starch to counterbalance the prevailing meats, fish and vegetables. Pink Firs (also known as Pink Fir Apples) are waxy, knobbly potatoes with a dusky pink skin, and they have a wonderful nutty flavour. It is important not to overcook them, because you really do want to hang onto their firm texture.

For four:
200g Pink Fir potatoes, well washed
Fine salt
1 head of chicory
Handful of dill, fronds picked and chopped
1 tablespoon small capers, drained
4 tablespoons Dill Dressing – see page 149

Place the Pink Firs in a pan and cover with cold water. Add a good pinch of fine salt and place over a high heat. Once boiled, reduce the heat to a lively simmer. Cook till al dente, about 15 minutes, then drain and set aside to cool.

When they are cool enough to handle, cut the potatoes on an angle into 1cm-thick slices. Cut the chicory in half and remove the core. Slice on an angle into 1cm slices. Place the potato, chicory, dill and capers in a large salad bowl. Pour in the dressing and mix well. Serve immediately.

Smoked Trout, Chicory & Dill Salad

I have always admired trout. They have a lot in common with their close relatives salmon, of course, but for me trout are more understated and, ultimately, classier. It seems almost in poor taste to observe that I prefer eating them, too. The very pale pink flesh strikes the perfect balance between butteriness and earthy sweetness. I am fortunate that my local fishmonger sells home-hickory-smoked trout, but you can get decent smoked fish at the supermarket fish counter these days.

For four:
2 heads of chicory
200g smoked trout
100g rocket, washed
4 sprigs of dill, fronds picked and finely chopped
4 tablespoons Dill Dressing – see page 149

Cut the chicory in half lengthways and remove the core. Slice on an angle into small pieces, wash in cold water and spin well in a salad spinner.

Gently flake the trout and place in a mixing bowl with the rocket, the chopped dill and the chicory. Add the dressing and carefully turn everything over a few times.

Pea, Feta & Radish Salad

When this salad first appeared on the menu I developed
a bit of a crush on it. It was so fresh, delicate and tasty that
barely a day went by without me eating one. Like the best
recipes, it uses only a handful of ingredients and lets them
speak for themselves.

Only use the freshest peas (found between June and
August in the UK) and the smallest mint leaves. In my
experience, radish leaves are usually thrown away, but they
really shouldn't be: they are soft and peppery, and deserve
their place on the plate.

For four:
200g podded peas
1 baby gem lettuce, washed
6 breakfast radishes, washed (retain the leaves)
1 shallot, finely diced
Small handful of mint leaves, cut into small strips
50g feta, crumbled
6 tablespoons Lemon Mustard Dressing – see page 146

If your peas are young and small, you should use them raw. If they are
any bigger than that, blanch them by putting them into rolling boiling
water for 30 seconds and then plunging them into iced water (a bowl
of water with ice cubes). Drain well and set aside.

Discard the stalk of the lettuce, and slice the leaves. Finely slice
the radishes using a French peeler (one that is swivel-headed).

Place the lettuce and sliced radish into a large mixing bowl with
the shallot, peas, mint, radish leaves and crumbled feta. Pour in
the dressing, mix well and serve immediately.

Beetroot, Soft-boiled Egg & Anchovy Salad

The difference between white anchovies (fresh from the fishmonger or marinated from a delicatessen) and the brown, bony variety you get in a flat tin is so marked that they are like different fish. Italians even have separate names for them. It's *alici* for the former, *acciughe* for the latter. Marinated white anchovy fillets are fine as tapas snacks or in salads – but there is no substitute for that intense hit you get from the tinned version. We are in deep saline territory here. My favourite brand is Ortiz – wonderful flavour and beautiful packaging.

For six:
500g small beetroot
2 teaspoons fine salt
2 teaspoons caster sugar
50ml red wine vinegar
6 medium eggs
6 tablespoons Sherry Vinegar Dressing - see page 150
2 shallots, finely sliced
250g watercress, leaves picked and washed
Flaky sea salt
1 x 50g tin of brown anchovies in olive oil

First, trim the beetroots and wash them. Place them in a saucepan and cover with water. Add the fine salt, the caster sugar and the red wine vinegar. Bring to the boil and reduce the heat to medium. Keep an eye on the water level and top up if necessary to keep the beetroots covered. Cook for about 45 minutes to an hour, depending on their size. The best way to test whether a beetroot is done is to poke it with a sharp knife; if there is no give, it is ready.

Once the beetroots are cooked, remove them from the heat and drain. While they are still warm, peel them. It's a messy job so it is best to use gloves. Then, cut them into quarters, place in a large bowl and set aside.

Bring a pan of water to the boil, add the eggs and boil for 6½ minutes, then transfer them to iced water (a bowl of water with ice cubes). Once the eggs have cooled down, gently peel them and set aside.

Add the dressing to the bowl of beetroots along with the shallots and the watercress. Turn all the ingredients over a few times to coat everything really well, add a little crunch of sea salt (not too much – the anchovies are fairly salty) and then divide equally onto six large plates. Drain the anchovies and slice them in half lengthways. Cut the eggs in half and lay them onto the salad along with the sliced anchovies.

Puntarelle, Fennel & Anchovy Salad

A lovely winter salad ingredient, from the chicory family, the long, serrated leaves of puntarelle are best picked young and bear more than a passing resemblance to dandelion. The flavour is subtle, slightly bitter, and the white core of the stems has a soft bite with a slightly crunchy texture. The classic Roman preparation is with an emulsified anchovy dressing, so this dish has its roots in tradition. Try to buy the youngest head of puntarelle that you can – the leaves will be tenderer. If they are small, buy two.

For four:
1 head of puntarelle
1 fennel bulb
1 shallot, finely sliced
25g small capers
4 tablespoons Anchovy Dressing - see page 151

Cut the base off the puntarelle and discard. Slice the leaves on an angle into 3cm pieces. Wash well in iced water (a bowl of water with ice cubes) and dry in a salad spinner. Take care that you do not damage the leaves by being too enthusiastic with the spinner. Gently does it. (If you don't have a salad spinner, incidentally, you could use a centrifugal tea-towel. Simply put the leaves into a clean tea-towel, loosely close the corners, and spin above your head.)

Cut the tips and base off the fennel and slice very thinly on a mandoline.

Place the puntarelle, fennel, shallot and capers into a large salad bowl. Pour in the anchovy dressing, mix well and serve immediately.

Green Bean, Feta & Hazelnut Salad

It is a minor irony, in these carbon-footprint-conscious times, that most of the 'French beans' you can buy in supermarkets come from Kenya. It is always a pleasure when summer arrives and home-grown green beans and bobby beans hit the grocer's shelves.

Bobby beans are slightly thicker than green beans and a good deal brighter too – their fresh, vibrant green colour becomes even more distinct when the beans are blanched.

For four to six:
50g shelled hazelnuts
1 teaspoon caraway seeds
1 teaspoon cumin seeds
1 teaspoon coriander seeds
1 teaspoon black sesame seeds
Flaky sea salt and black pepper
Fine salt
250g green or bobby beans, stalk ends trimmed
100g rocket
100g feta, broken up into bite-sized pieces
4 tablespoons Lemon Mustard Dressing – see page 146

Put the hazelnuts in a non-stick pan and dry fry over a medium heat for a few minutes until they are golden. Remove from the pan and allow to cool. Put the caraway, cumin and coriander seeds into the same pan and dry fry over a medium heat for a few minutes until you can smell their spiciness. Do keep an eye on them, as they can easily burn. Remove the seeds from the heat, then grind in a pestle and mortar. Now put the black sesame seeds in the same pan and toast them in the same way. Do not grind these.

Mix together the toasted hazelnuts, and all the ground and unground seeds, plus a pinch of flaky salt and a twist of black pepper.

Put a saucepan of water over a high heat, add some fine salt, and bring to the boil. Add the beans, and continue to boil gently until the beans are al dente but not too crunchy, about 3-4 minutes. Undercooked beans have a tendency to be a bit squeaky and that's not very pleasant. Drain the beans and run under cold water to stop them cooking. Drain well.

When the beans have cooled a little, place them in a mixing bowl with the rocket, crumbled feta, hazelnut and black sesame mix. Pour in the dressing, mix well and serve immediately.

Asparagus, Soft-boiled Egg & Hazelnut Salad

When English asparagus comes into season around St George's Day, there is usually a bit of a frenzy amongst the London fooderati. Some very early-season spears inevitably pop up on menus in March, but nowhere near so delicious as the stuff that arrives with spring proper. Poetically, the asparagus season traditionally ends on Midsummer's Day. Incidentally, there is an etymological myth that the word comes from 'sparrowgrass'. The very opposite is true. It was probably corrupted to 'sparrowgrass' in the seventeenth century and persisted until the late nineteenth century.
I think I would like to start a campaign for its resurrection.

For four:
50g shelled hazelnuts
1 teaspoon caraway seeds
1 teaspoon cumin seeds
1 teaspoon coriander seeds
1 teaspoon black sesame seeds
Flaky sea salt and black pepper
4 small eggs
Fine salt
At least 20 spears of slender English asparagus
1 head of frisée lettuce
100g lamb's leaf lettuce
½ bunch of spring onions, sliced thinly on an angle
6 tablespoons Vinaigrette – see page 147

Toast the hazelnuts and the seeds as in the previous recipe. Mix together the toasted hazelnuts, and all the ground and unground seeds, plus a pinch of flaky salt and a twist of black pepper. Bring a pan of water to the boil, add the eggs and boil for 6½ minutes, then transfer to iced water (a bowl of water with ice cubes). Once the eggs have cooled down, gently peel them and set them aside.

Bring another pan of water to the boil, and generously add fine salt. Break the woody ends off the asparagus and discard them, then cut the spears at an angle. Once the water has started to boil, drop the asparagus into the pan and boil fully for no more than 2 minutes. Drain, plunge into iced water as above and set aside.

Remove the core from the frisée and cut the leaves into four, wash in iced water as above and dry in a salad spinner. Place in a deep bowl with the lamb's leaf, asparagus and spring onions and pour in the dressing. Mix well and transfer to four large plates. Cut the eggs in half and arrange on top, generously scattering with the hazelnut and black sesame mix. Serve immediately.

Zucchini, Dandelion & Lovage Salad

Here is a salad that can come mostly from your garden, if you are lucky enough to have one. Dandelion you'll find almost anywhere. Lovage is a perennial herb that grows enthusiastically and is a lovely, fresh salad and soup ingredient. It resembles flat parsley and has a flavour reminiscent of celery. If you don't grow it yourself, you'll probably find it at a farmers' market.

Make sure you wash and dry the leaves of both plants well. It will greatly improve the look of the salad if you can get your hands on a green and a yellow zucchini. Pick young dandelion leaves, not old ones.

For four:
2 zucchini (aka courgettes), washed
200g dandelion leaves, washed
Small handful of lovage leaves, washed
4 tablespoons Lemon Mustard Dressing – see page 146

Trim the ends off both zucchini and, using a mandoline or a French peeler, slice very thinly into ribbons. Cut the dandelion into 2cm lengths, slice the lovage very thinly and then combine the two and wash in cold water. Drain and dry in a salad spinner and place in a bowl with the zucchini.

Add the dressing, turn a few times with your hands and serve straightaway.

Butternut, Rainbow Chard & Taleggio

The beautiful colours in rainbow chard always cheer me up. It is reassuring that nature can effortlessly produce such natural vibrancy and satisfying, too, that the cooking process does not diminish it. Combining rainbow chard with butternut squash and Taleggio makes for a really compelling ensemble of warm, earthy flavours, but also results in a dish that is so visually striking it wouldn't be out of place in an art gallery.

For four:
1 small butternut squash
Small handful of sage leaves
2 garlic cloves, finely chopped
Flaky sea salt and black pepper
Extra virgin olive oil
Fine salt
1 bunch of rainbow chard, about 200g, thoroughly washed
200g Taleggio, thinly sliced

Preheat the oven to 200°C/Gas 6.

Cut the butternut in half lengthways, scoop out the seeds, then cut the flesh into small to medium 'chips'. Place in a large bowl with the sage leaves, one of the chopped garlic cloves, a few very good pinches of sea salt, a twist of black pepper, and 2 tablespoons of olive oil. Turn everything over a few times with your hands to coat the butternut thoroughly, then transfer to a baking tray and put the tray into the oven. After 10 minutes, turn the pieces of butternut over and cook for a further 10 minutes.

Meanwhile prepare the rainbow chard. Place a pan of salted water over a high heat and bring to the boil. Separate the leaves and the stems. Cut the stems diagonally into bite-sized strips. Cut the leaves into quarters. Once the water has come to the boil add the stems and cook for 1 minute, then add the leaves and boil for a further 30 seconds. Remove from the water and squeeze out any excess liquid. Place into a large mixing bowl and add a good few glugs of olive oil, a pinch of salt and pepper and the remaining chopped garlic clove. Turn several times to coat the chard well.

Once the butternut comes out of the oven, place the chard on top and then slices of Taleggio. Return to the oven for 2 minutes so that the cheese has just started to melt.

Carefully transfer to serving plates. This lovely warm salad is best eaten immediately.

Dressings

In my kitchen, beside my stove, I keep a small arsenal of condiments. There are a dozen or so bottles that get a varying degree of love. If I'm being honest, I can't remember the last time I used the Marsala, and the balsamic vinegar has fallen out of favour of late. But the extra virgin olive oil is used on an almost daily basis, and my bottle of bog-standard vegetable oil gets regular outings too.

The two bottles that really stand out, however, are my expensive extra virgin olive oil and my fancy white wine vinegar. These are the ones I reach for when I am making a salad dressing. I do recommend treating yourself to a super-quality olive oil, perhaps cold-pressed and from a renowned estate. It will give your dressings an edge, particularly if married with excellent white wine vinegar. I like single grape variety vinegars – I often use chardonnay vinegar.

For the majority of dressings in this section I employ the tried-and-tested 'lo-fi' method with an old jam jar. I like Bonne Maman jars, which have a very tight-fitting lid, a wide mouth, and, at 324ml, are the perfect size too.

The method is simple: put all the ingredients into the jar, close the lid tightly and then, over the kitchen sink, shake it like a maniac. You will find that 30 seconds of vigorous shaking completely combines the oil and vinegar and emulsifies the dressing.

Many of the recipes make 200ml or so which, for six people, allows about 2 tablespoons of dressing each – a good amount. But if you have leftovers, don't panic, as all these dressings will keep very well in the fridge for up to a week.

Lemon Mustard Dressing

This is a bright and zingy dressing that will liven up even the most prosaic leaf.

Makes 200ml:
1 generous tablespoon Dijon mustard
25ml red wine vinegar
25ml lemon juice
150ml extra virgin olive oil
1 teaspoon flaky sea salt
Large pinch of black pepper

Put everything into a clean, empty jam jar, close the lid tightly, and shake enthusiastically for 30 seconds or more.

Vinaigrette

There is contention in my household over the provenance of this vinaigrette recipe. My wife Jules claims it's hers. I feel like I have always known it. It doesn't really matter since it's a classic French provincial staple that has been around for centuries. (The addition of that pinch of sugar makes all the difference, by the way. Don't forget it.)

Makes about 275ml:
½ garlic clove, very finely chopped
Flaky sea salt and black pepper
½ teaspoon caster sugar
2 tablespoons Dijon mustard
200ml extra virgin olive oil
70ml red wine vinegar

Put the chopped garlic into an empty, clean jam jar with a good pinch of sea salt, a good twist of pepper and the caster sugar. Add the mustard, oil and vinegar and close the lid tightly. Shake vigorously for at least 30 seconds. This will keep for up to a week in the fridge. Remember to remove it from the fridge half an hour before you want to use it – it tends to thicken somewhat at low temperatures. Give it another shake before using.

Shallot Vinaigrette

If I am eating a very simple salad comprised of one type of lettuce and nothing else, I will often dress it with shallot vinaigrette to lend a little bit of texture and a subtle sweetness. The vinaigrette is delicious on Castelfranco, a fine-leafed radicchio native to the commune of the same name just north of Treviso in Veneto. Its leaves are a very soft creamy yellow with distinctive red speckles, and it grows in concentric circles like a rose. It has a season of approximately five months from November to March, and needs to be handled carefully because of its fragility, so take care not to crease or crush the leaves.

Makes 200ml:
150ml extra virgin olive oil
50ml red wine vinegar
2 teaspoons Dijon mustard
1 garlic clove, finely chopped
1 shallot, finely diced
Flaky sea salt and black pepper

In a clean, empty jam jar put the olive oil, vinegar, mustard, garlic, shallot and a good pinch each of salt and pepper. Close the lid very tightly and shake vigorously for 30 seconds or so.

Tarragon Dressing

A lovely variation on vinaigrette with a fresh, almost liquoricey flavour. It works particularly well on crunchy green lettuce such as baby gem or Romaine and is essential for a good chopped salad (see page 116).

Makes about 200ml:
Small handful of tarragon leaves
2 teaspoons Dijon mustard
25ml white wine vinegar
25ml cold water
150ml extra virgin olive oil
Flaky sea salt and black pepper

Finely chop the tarragon and put it into an empty, clean jam jar along with the mustard, vinegar, water and olive oil. Add a good pinch of sea salt and a twist of black pepper. Place the lid on very tightly and vigorously shake the jar for 30 seconds until all the ingredients have combined.

Dill Dressing

As well as being perky and fragrant in its own right, this dressing is an excellent accompaniment to fish. It goes very well with hot-smoked salmon and I often use it to dress warm new potatoes, too.

Makes about 210ml:
Small handful of dill, fronds picked
2 teaspoons Dijon mustard
2 teaspoons white wine vinegar
Juice of 1 small lemon
150ml extra virgin olive oil
2 teaspoons cold water
1 teaspoon flaky sea salt
½ teaspoon black pepper

Chop the dill very finely indeed and put it into an empty, clean jam jar with the mustard, vinegar, lemon juice, olive oil and water. Add the salt and pepper, close the lid firmly and shake vigorously until the ingredients come together into a gloriously silky gloop.

Sherry Vinegar Dressing

This dressing has a very grown-up character. It is excellent
for lending a salad a bit of gravitas, and works well with
warm ingredients.

Makes 200ml:
Flaky sea salt and black pepper
½ teaspoon caster sugar
1 garlic clove
50ml sherry vinegar
150ml extra virgin olive oil

Put a good pinch of salt, a good twist of black pepper and the caster
sugar into an empty, clean jam jar. With a very sharp knife, finely chop
the garlic into the smallest pieces you can manage. Add to the jar
along with the vinegar and olive oil. Place the lid on very tightly
and vigorously shake the jar for 30 seconds until all the ingredients
have combined.

Walnut Dressing

A bold and robust dressing that needs to be treated with
respect – it can overpower lesser ingredients. Use it alongside
other strong flavours, such as the Blood Orange, Walnut &
Ricotta Salata Salad on page 129.

Makes 200ml:
2 teaspoons Dijon mustard
25ml sherry vinegar
Good pinch of flaky sea salt
½ teaspoon black pepper
150ml walnut oil
25ml cold water

Place the mustard, vinegar, salt and pepper into an empty, clean jam jar
with the oil and water. Close the lid firmly and shake hard.

Anchovy Dressing

It is very easy to get carried away with this dressing. Left to my own devices, I could happily pour it onto just about anything.

Makes about 210ml:
1 small egg yolk
2 teaspoons Dijon mustard
1 generous tablespoon red wine vinegar
30g brown anchovies, drained of oil (reserve the oil for later)
½ garlic clove, finely chopped
Tabasco sauce
Flaky sea salt and black pepper
150ml sunflower oil
2 teaspoons water
2 teaspoons lemon juice

This is a good time to use that stick blender if you have one. If you don't, then a food processor will do. Place the egg yolk, mustard, vinegar, anchovies and garlic into a bowl or food processor. Add a few dashes of Tabasco and a good pinch each of salt and pepper. Blend to combine. Now, with the motor still running, slowly drizzle in the leftover anchovy oil, then the sunflower oil, and lastly the water and lemon juice.

Delta Dressing

This is a perky sauce to liven up seafood and crunchy salad. You could play around with the quantities of Tabasco if you like it spicier.

For four to six:
1 egg yolk, beaten
1 bunch of spring onions, washed and very finely chopped
1 pickled onion, very finely chopped
1 teaspoon lemon juice
1 teaspoon Dijon mustard
1 teaspoon Horseradish Cream – in the recipe for
    Mackerel Slider, see page 174
1 generous tablespoon tomato ketchup
10 shakes of Tabasco sauce
5 shakes of Worcestershire sauce
100ml olive oil
Good pinch of paprika
Pinch of flaky sea salt

Put all the ingredients into a clean jam jar, close the lid tightly, and shake vigorously until all the ingredients are combined.

Mayonnaise

I would encourage you to make your own mayonnaise if you
have the time. It's one of those very satisfying and therapeutic
kitchen activities. If you don't have the time or the inclination,
however, there is no shame in using shop-bought mayonnaise,
which I do, often.

This recipe makes quite a lot of mayo, but it keeps well.
You can also make it by hand, in one or two egg yolk quantities,
scaling down the ingredients accordingly. Place the yolks and
other ingredients in a bowl and mix using a balloon whisk.
Add the oil a drop at a time to begin with, then as a trickle,
whisking all the while.

Makes 600ml:
3 medium egg yolks
2 scant teaspoons flaky sea salt
Pinch of black pepper
3½ tablespoons Dijon mustard
25ml white wine vinegar
450ml vegetable oil
50ml water

Place the egg yolks, salt, pepper, mustard and vinegar into a food
processor and blend to combine. With the motor still running, carefully
add the vegetable oil in a steady, slow stream and then the water,
likewise. Transfer to a sealable jar or container, where it will keep
for up to a week.

To make an aïoli, a garlicky mayonnaise, simply add a finely chopped
clove of garlic and a tablespoon of lemon juice to the basic mayonnaise
at the first stage. To make a Tabasco mayonnaise, add 12 shakes of
Tabasco sauce to the aïoli at the first stage.

Little Italy, NoLIta, SoHo

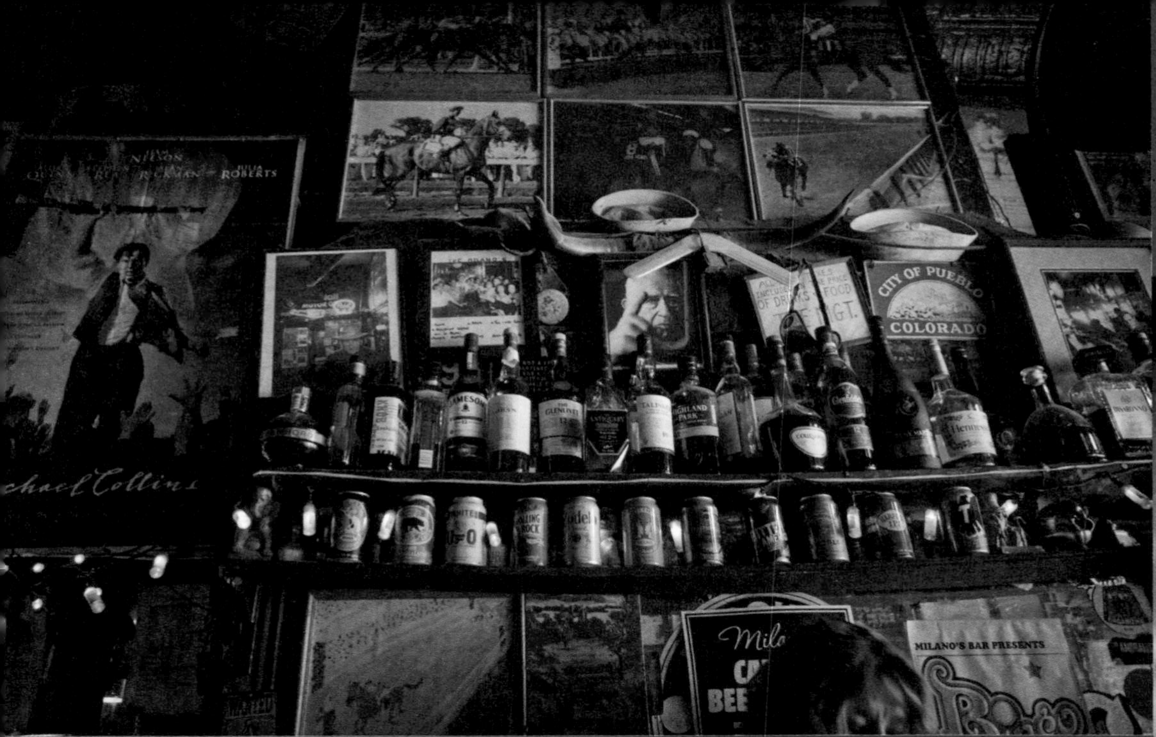
CITY OF PUEBLO
COLORADO
MILANO'S BAR PRESENTS

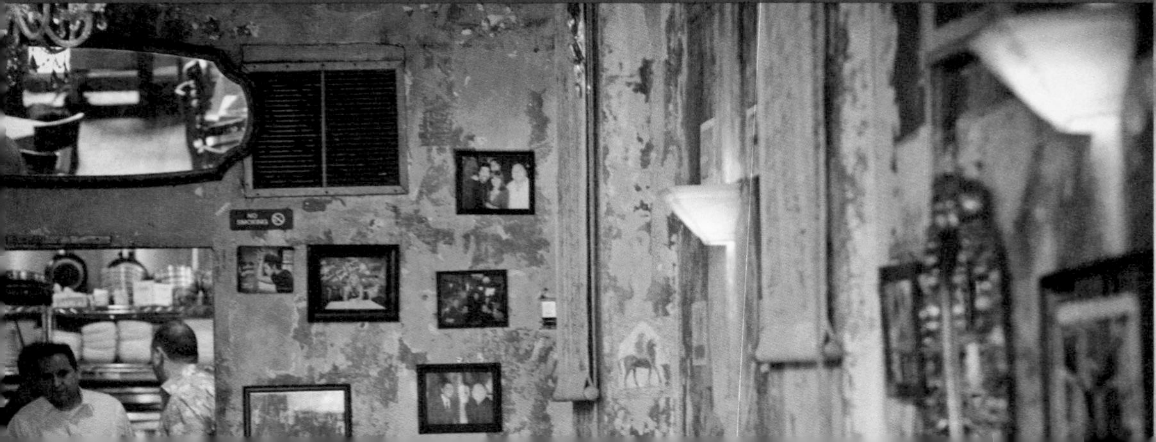

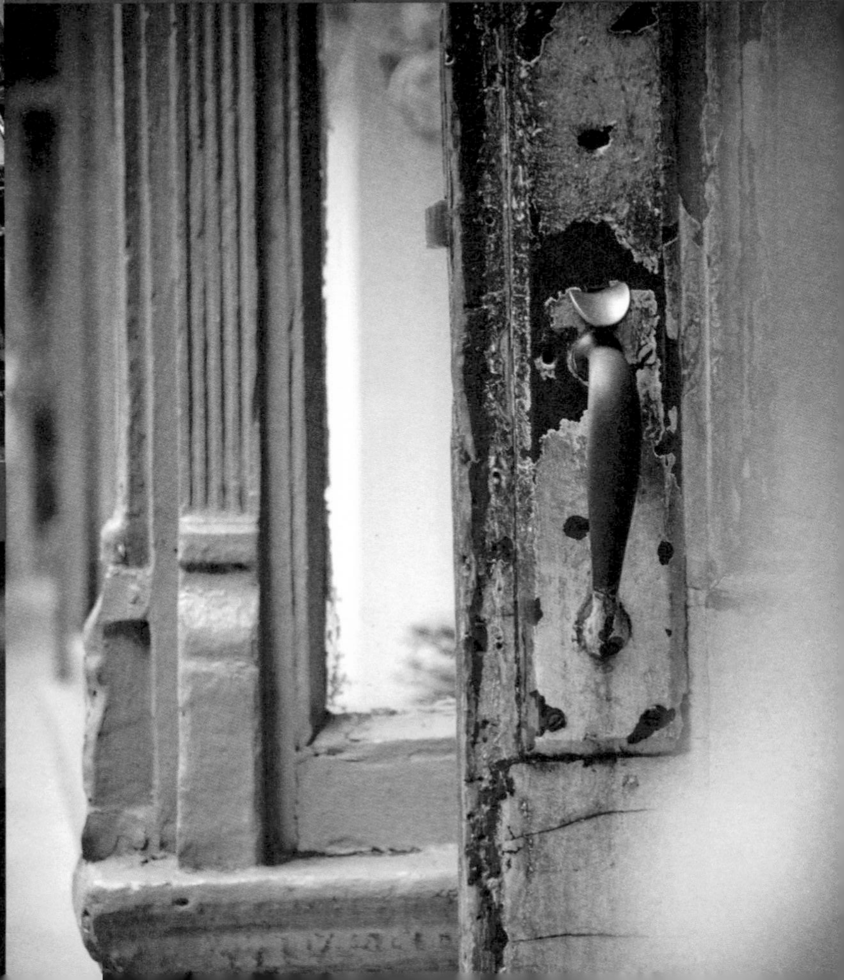

Sliders

What is a slider? Well, it might be useful to start by saying what a slider is not: it is not just a mini-burger. It is true that White Castle, the fast-food chain that is credited with creating the first slider in the 1920s, made their influential patty as simply a smaller, square version of the standard burger. But since then the term 'slider' has come to be associated more with the small bun than its contents. Sliders these days can, and do, contain all manner of fillings. Can you put anything into a slider? Probably not. There may not be hard and fast rules, but my instinct is to assume the innards need to consist of a patty or a meatball or suchlike.

Being a frequent and greedy visitor to New York I am struck by the many different types of slider you find. Kenny Shopsin at his eccentric diner in Essex Street Market likes the White Castle formula, served with processed cheese in square buns that are still connected to each other at the edges. (They are excellent, by the way.) Andrew Carmellini over at Locanda Verde makes a lamb meatball slider that is elegant and refined. (But equally delicious.) Keith McNally's Schiller's Liquor Bar serves them up sloppy with onions. (Also great.) At SPUNTINO our patties are relatively large at 2½ ounces, or 70 grams. The brioche bun gives them a nice height and we lance them with a wooden skewer.

Incidentally, I have heard a few tales as to how sliders got their name. Some people believe they are so-called because the chef would slide them across the pass from grill to counter. Others insist it's because they slide down your gullet so easily. I have even come across an implausible explanation that they were cooked on navy ships in the 1940s for sailors, and the greasy little patties would slide back and forth with the pitch of the ships on the ocean. Ridiculous.

Brioche Buns

So often when I order a burger or a slider in a restaurant
it is clear that a lot of thought has gone into the provenance
of the meat, the length of time for which it has been aged,
the grade of the grind used to create the mince, the seasoning
to enhance its flavour, the exact method of grilling and the
condiments that go with it. But too often the bun has been
overlooked.

A good bun is an essential part of a good burger. It should
be soft, but not so soft that it disintegrates when the meat
juices soak through it. It should be squidgy enough to push
down onto the meat, but firm enough to hold when you lift
it to your mouth. And it should have a slight sweetness to
balance the deep savoury flavours of the patty.

You can pop the buns cut-side down on a hot griddle
if you want to warm them through before filling and serving.

For twenty-four slider buns or twelve burger buns:
230ml warm water
2 tablespoons tepid milk
20g fresh yeast or 10g fast-action yeast
2½ tablespoons caster sugar
2 medium eggs
500g strong white bread flour, plus extra for dusting
1½ teaspoons fine salt
40g unsalted butter, softened at room temperature

Mix together the warm water, milk, fresh yeast and sugar. Leave
the mixture to stand for about 5 minutes until it is foamy.

Meanwhile, beat one of the eggs. Place the flour, salt and butter
into a large mixing bowl and rub the ingredients together until they
resemble breadcrumbs. (If using instant yeast sprinkle it over the
mixture now and stir well.) Add the beaten egg and the foamy yeast
mix and work everything into a dough with your hands. Tip out onto
a lightly floured surface and knead for 10 minutes, until the dough is
smooth and springy.

Shape the dough into a ball and place back in the bowl, draping a damp
cloth or oiled clingfilm over it. Leave in a warm place to allow the dough
to double in size. This will take about an hour.

Line a baking tray with greased parchment paper. Divide the dough
into twelve 70g pieces for burgers or twenty-four 35g pieces for sliders.

On a lightly floured surface roll the dough into balls, and gently place them on the baking tray, leaving a few centimetres between them. Cover loosely with oiled clingfilm and leave in a warm place to rise for an hour or so.

Preheat the oven to 180°C/Gas 4.

Once the buns are ready to go into the oven, beat the remaining egg with a splash of water and gently brush over the buns. Place a shallow tray on the bottom shelf and pour into it about a teacup of water to make some steam. Place the buns in the middle of the preheated oven and bake for 15-25 minutes, depending on their size, till golden brown. Transfer to a wire rack to cool.

Lamb Meatball Slider

Lamb is such a soft, sweet meat. I find it almost fragrant at times. In the culinary landscape of the burger and slider, the cow is the dominant beast, but it is good to stray occasionally. These meatballs are enhanced by aromatic rosemary and fennel, and further benefit from a generous spoonful of tomato sauce and a rather subtle and sophisticated pickle.

For six sliders:
Extra virgin olive oil
½ onion, finely diced
½ garlic clove, finely chopped
½ fennel bulb, cored and finely diced
4 sprigs of rosemary, leaves picked and chopped
400g finely ground lamb mince
1 teaspoon ground fennel seeds
1 teaspoon tomato paste
1 teaspoon Dijon mustard
1 medium egg
15g fresh breadcrumbs
Flaky sea salt and black pepper
100ml Basic Tomato Sauce – see page 89
6 Brioche Buns, slider size – see page 160

For the pickled cucumber:
½ medium cucumber
½ tablespoon caster sugar
½ teaspoon fine salt

Place a pan over a very low heat, add a glug of olive oil and gently sauté the onion, garlic, fennel and rosemary, stirring every minute or so to prevent the mixture from catching, and otherwise keeping covered with a lid. After about 15 minutes, when the mixture is really soft, transfer to a small bowl and allow to cool.

Place the lamb mince, ground fennel, tomato paste, Dijon mustard, egg and breadcrumbs in a large mixing bowl. Once the onion mixture has cooled, add to the large bowl and mix everything together thoroughly. Add a pinch of salt and pepper and turn a few more times. Roll the mixture into six equal balls and refrigerate for an hour.

While the lamb is resting in the fridge, you can prepare the pickle. Cut the cucumber crossways into thin slices and place in a small plastic container with a sealable lid. Add the sugar and salt and stir to make sure each piece is coated. Close the lid and refrigerate for at least half an hour.

Now, place the meatballs on an oiled tray, roll around to coat them in oil, and then flatten them slightly. Preheat the oven to 180°C/Gas 4 while the meatballs lose their fridge chill. Bake for 20-25 minutes or until browned and cooked through. Meanwhile heat the tomato sauce in a small saucepan.

Split the brioche buns, and place a meatball in each with a good tablespoon of tomato sauce and a few pieces of the pickled cucumber. Spike each bun with a large wooden skewer.

Beef & Bone-marrow Slider

This is SPUNTINO's most popular slider. We sometimes sell more than a hundred in a day. The reason for its popularity is almost certainly the bone marrow. It adds an indulgent depth of flavour and a silky texture that you rarely get with common-or-garden hamburgers.

Marrow can be extracted from the larger bones of any big animal, but we tend to use veal. You can buy the whole sections yourself and dig out the marrow with a long, thin spoon, or you can ask your kind butcher to do it for you. For the minced beef, my preference is for shin.

For six sliders:
Extra virgin olive oil
½ onion, finely diced
1 heaped teaspoon oregano leaves, chopped
½ garlic clove, finely chopped
Flaky sea salt and black pepper
400g good-quality beef mince
50g bone marrow, removed from bones, diced
1 teaspoon tomato purée
1 medium egg, beaten
15g fresh breadcrumbs
6 slices of Gruyère
6 Brioche Buns, slider size – see page 160
1 shallot, very thinly sliced
6 small cornichons, very thinly sliced

Place a heavy-based saucepan over a low heat with a glug of olive oil and sweat the onion, oregano and garlic on the lowest heat until very soft. This should take about 10–15 minutes of stirring occasionally to prevent catching. Add a pinch of sea salt and a twist of black pepper. When soft and translucent, remove from the heat, transfer to a large bowl and allow to cool.

Preheat the oven to 180°C/Gas 4. When the mixture has cooled, add the mince, bone marrow, tomato purée, egg and breadcrumbs to the bowl, and mix and season well. Roll into six equal balls, making sure the bone marrow is democratically represented in each patty.

Place them on an oiled baking tray and flatten them slightly. Bake in the preheated oven for 15–18 minutes, or until cooked through.

Remove the tray from the oven and place a slice of Gruyère onto each patty and then put the tray back in the oven for no more than 2 minutes to melt the cheese.

Cut the brioche buns in half. Top the base of each bun with a few shallot slices, then place a patty on each. Scatter over the cornichons. Lance each slider with a large wooden skewer.

Salt Beef Slider

The lure of salt beef (UK) or corned beef (US) has led me on some rather elaborate journeys in order to get my fix. In London there are relatively few old-school salt beef sandwich joints – an Oxford Street department store food hall, a Brick Lane bagel shop, an East London street market – whereas in New York you are fairly spoilt for choice. The crown of Corned Beef King is variously claimed by Katz's, Barney Greengrass, Second Avenue Deli and Carnegie Deli, to name just a few.

The classic salt beef sandwich, of course, consists of salted brisket cut thick, served between two slices of rye bread with pickle and mustard. Like all classics, you don't mess with the formula. At SPUNTINO we simply put it in a slider bun.

For six sliders:
500g salted brisket of beef
½ bottle white wine
2 bay leaves
6 black peppercorns
1 large onion, roughly cut
2 carrots, roughly cut
3 celery sticks, roughly cut
6 Brioche Buns, slider size – see page 160
Colman's English mustard (or French's American Classic mustard
    if you prefer it less strong)
At least 4 large gherkins, finely sliced lengthways

Trim all sinew from the salt beef and most of the fat, and rinse under cold water. Place in a large pan, add the wine, bay leaves, peppercorns, onion, carrot and celery, and top up with enough cold water to cover the brisket. Make sure the meat is submerged completely. You can place a plate on top to keep it under the surface.

Bring to the boil and then reduce to a medium-low heat so that the liquid is just simmering. Cover and cook for about 3 hours, until the meat is just falling apart.

Carefully lift the brisket out of the pan and place it on a chopping board to rest for 15 minutes.

Split the brioche buns in half and generously spread some mustard on the bottom half. With a very sharp knife, divide the brisket into sixths. Place the salt beef chunks on the bottom brioche halves and top with a few slices of gherkin and some more mustard. Close the sliders and carefully push a wooden skewer through each one to help stabilise them. If you like, you can serve with extra pickles and more mustard on the side.

Ox Tongue, Pickled Beet & Horseradish Slider

Ox tongue is one of those cuts that divides opinion. On the one hand, it is a consistently firm meat with a distinctively rich flavour. On the other hand it looks so, well, like a tongue, I suppose. Perhaps this dish might just cure you of any lingering squeamishness.

Tongue requires a little preparation and a long cooking time to achieve the required tenderness. You will need to start your preparations at least a week before eating.

For six sliders:
1 ox tongue
Olive oil
A knob of unsalted butter
6 Brioche Buns, slider size – see page 160
50g Horseradish Cream – in the recipe for Mackerel Slider, see page 174
6 slices of Beetroot Pickle, finely sliced – see page 76

For the brine:
500g caster sugar
300g coarse sea salt
12 juniper berries
12 cloves
10 black peppercorns
6 bay leaves

For the cooking liquid:
2 onions, peeled and halved
3 carrots, peeled and quartered
2 celery sticks, cut into thirds
1 head of garlic, cut in half horizontally
12 peppercorns
Small handful of thyme leaves
Small handful of sage leaves
4 bay leaves

Put the brine ingredients into a very large saucepan and add around 4 litres of cold water. Stir several times and turn the heat up high. Just as the liquid starts to boil, remove the pan from the heat and allow it to cool completely to room temperature. Transfer to a large plastic Tupperware container and submerge the ox tongue in the brine, placing a plate on top so that it is completely covered. Leave in the fridge for seven to ten days.

A week or so later, and ideally a day before eating, remove the ox tongue from the brine, place it in a colander and wash it thoroughly under cold running water.

Place the ox tongue in a large saucepan with the ingredients for the cooking liquid and cover with water. Gently bring to the boil, reduce the heat to a simmer, cover and cook for 3½ hours.

Lift the ox tongue out of the cooking liquid and while it is still hot remove and discard the outer layer of skin. You might want to wear gloves to do this to protect your hands from the heat. Set the tongue aside to cool. (NB: the tongue may be larger than you need for six sliders so make sure you retain the cooking liquid to submerge the remainder in the sealed plastic container for storage in the fridge. It is delicious sliced thinly and served cold as you would a ham, and it keeps for a week or so.)

When the tongue has completely cooled, starting from the thin end, cut off twelve x 1cm-thick slices. Place a frying pan on a medium heat and add a splash of olive oil and the knob of butter. Once the butter has melted, gently fry the tongue slices on both sides until just turning brown, no more than a couple of minutes.

Cut the brioche buns in half. Top the base bun with a generous dollop of horseradish cream and divide the pickled beetroot equally. Place two slices of fried tongue on this and cover with the bun top. Skewer with a wooden lance and serve.

Beef Cheek, Celeriac & Chipotle Slider

How I love beef cheeks. They are a particularly lean cut, as
you might expect from muscles that do all that rumination,
but also incredibly tough, and they need slow cooking in order
to render them tender. The result is meat that is so yielding
that you should be able to cut it with the edge of your fork.

For six sliders:
500g beef cheeks
1 onion, roughly chopped
2 carrots, roughly chopped
2 celery sticks, roughly chopped
4 sprigs of rosemary
6 bay leaves
Zest of 1 orange
10 black peppercorns
1 bottle red wine
2 litres chicken stock
100g plain flour, for dredging
Fine salt
Knob of butter
Olive oil
6 Brioche Buns, slider size – see page 160

For the celeriac rémoulade:
¼ celeriac, cut into matchsticks
Juice of ½ lemon
Flaky sea salt
100g Mayonnaise – see page 152
100g crème fraîche
20g chipotle chilli paste

Remove and discard the sinew and silvery skin from the meat and place
the meat in a large plastic container with the chopped vegetables, the
herbs, the zest and the peppercorns. Pour over the red wine, seal with
a lid and refrigerate for 24 hours.

The next day, lift the meat out of the marinade and set aside. Strain the
vegetables, retaining only the red wine. Place a large saucepan over a
medium heat and add the red wine and chicken stock. Bring to the boil
and then reduce to a simmer.

Meanwhile dredge the beef cheeks in flour seasoned with a good pinch
of salt and shake off any excess. Heat the butter and a glug of olive oil
in a large frying pan and fry the cheeks in batches over high heat until
browned on both sides. Now add the cheeks to the wine and stock, and
cover the pan. Simmer for 3 hours until the meat has no resistance.

While the beef cheeks are gently bubbling, make the celeriac rémoulade by combining the celeriac, lemon juice and salt in a plastic bowl. Mix them together well so that the matchsticks are coated and set aside for half an hour.

Remove the beef saucepan from the heat and lift the cheeks out of the liquid. Once they have completely cooled, using a very sharp knife, cut them into 2cm slices. You can pop them back into the cooking liquid to keep them warm while you add the mayonnaise, crème fraîche and chipotle paste to the resting celeriac. Mix the rémoulade well.

Cut the brioche buns in half and generously top with the celeriac mix and warmed beef cheek slices.

Oxtail, Mustard & Watercress Slider

Oxtail is another of those richly flavoured meats that make it difficult for me to contemplate life as a vegetarian. Like all the tastiest cuts you have to work hard to get the best from it. Here the effort mainly involves patience while it marinates – not too great a hardship. Because the cooked meat will be soft, sticky and deeply sweet, it requires nothing more than a spicy nudge from the mustard and a hint of pepper from the watercress.

For six sliders:
500g oxtail, cut into sections
1 onion, roughly chopped
3 carrots, roughly chopped
3 celery sticks, roughly chopped
1 head of garlic, cut in half horizontally
Small handful of thyme leaves
6 bay leaves
12 black peppercorns
A bottle of red wine
2 litres chicken stock
100g plain flour, seasoned with salt and pepper
Olive oil, for frying
6 Brioche Buns, slider size – see page 160
Dijon mustard
1 bunch of watercress, leaves picked and washed

Place the oxtail in a large sealable plastic container with the chopped vegetables, garlic, herbs and peppercorns. Pour in all the red wine and place a sheet of baking parchment on top. Weigh it down with a plate, close the lid, and refrigerate for 24 hours.

The next day, remove the oxtail from the marinade. Strain and discard the vegetables, retaining the red wine only. Add the red wine and chicken stock to a large saucepan and place over a medium to high heat.

Meanwhile dredge the oxtail pieces in the flour, and shake off any excess. Heat a good couple of glugs of olive oil in a frying pan, and fry the oxtail pieces in batches over a high heat until browned all over. Add to the saucepan with the wine, and cover the pan. Bring to the boil and reduce to a lowish heat, so that it is just ticking over. Cook for 3 hours, until the meat comes away from the bone without any resistance. Once cooked, lift the oxtail out of the stock, allow it to cool a little, and pick the meat off the bone while still warm.

Transfer 3-4 tablespoons of the wine stock to a frying pan and heat to a bubble. Place the picked meat in the liquid and reduce by half.

Cut the brioche buns in half and put a good smear of mustard, then some watercress on the bottom. Top with oxtail and the other half of the bun, lance with a wooden skewer and serve.

Mackerel Slider

Mackerel has a robustness of flavour that can easily stand its ground with bold accompaniments. In this combination, the horseradish and beetroot really do deliver a punch. Use only the freshest mackerel; in the fishmonger's you want to see bright, clear eyes and gleaming black stripes on the skin.

I suppose you could use horseradish cream from a jar but it's much more satisfying to make your own. These quantities will make more than you need, but it will keep for a week in the fridge and I'm sure you'll find an excuse to polish it off.

For six sliders:
500g skinless mackerel fillets
Flaky sea salt
1 medium egg, beaten
25g fresh breadcrumbs
Handful of mint leaves, finely chopped
1 teaspoon chilli flakes
1 garlic clove, finely chopped
Finely grated zest of 1 lemon
Juice of ½ lemon
6 Brioche Buns, slider size – see page 160

For the horseradish cream:
150g crème fraîche
25g fresh horseradish, finely grated (use the fine side of a cheese grater)
Pinch of cracked black pepper
½ teaspoon flaky sea salt
1 tablespoon lemon juice
1 teaspoon Dijon mustard

For the pickled red cabbage:
¼ small red cabbage, shredded
1 teaspoon fine salt
1 teaspoon caster sugar
1 teaspoon lemon juice

Wash the mackerel fillets under a cold running tap, making sure there are no traces of skin, bone or cartilage. Using a sharp knife, finely chop the mackerel.

Place the mackerel and all the remaining slider ingredients in a bowl and mix well. Roll into six balls of equal size and then flatten them slightly to make fat, round patties. Refrigerate for an hour.

To make the horseradish cream, place all of the ingredients into a large bowl and mix well. Set aside.

To make the pickled cabbage, mix the ingredients together in a sealable plastic container, close the lid and set aside for half an hour.

Meanwhile, preheat the oven to 180°C/Gas 4. Lightly oil a baking tray and place the refrigerated mackerel patties onto it. Allow them to come to room temperature and then bake in the preheated oven for 10-12 minutes, turning them over once.

Cut the brioche buns in half, and generously spread the horseradish cream onto both sides. Place a mackerel patty on each bottom half and top with the pickled cabbage before closing the buns and piercing each with a wooden skewer through the centre.

Prawn Po' Boy

My advice to purists would be to look away at this point and perhaps move on to the next recipe. At SPUNTINO we have always called this very popular slider our 'Prawn Po' Boy' – but it is not, dear reader, quite the genuine article.

The name 'po' boy' comes from Louisiana slang for 'poor boy', the term used for employees of a New Orleans streetcar company who went on strike for four months in 1929. The free sandwiches prepared by a local restaurant became synonymous with the strikers and were soon known as po' boys.

Traditionally a po' boy contains shredded beef or fried seafood, usually with lettuce and mayonnaise, served in a long, submarine-style sandwich. Ours falls short on its shape since we package it as a slider. I hope the pedants will continue to point out the error of our ways for years to come.

For six sliders:
2 medium eggs
1 teaspoon Dijon mustard
1 teaspoon paprika
100g plain flour, seasoned with salt and pepper
85g panko breadcrumbs – see page 62
18 medium prawns, shelled and deveined
700ml vegetable oil, for deep frying
6 Brioche Buns, slider size – see page 160
6 tablespoons Delta Dressing – see page 151
1 baby gem lettuce, washed and shredded

Whisk the eggs with the Dijon mustard and the paprika. Set up a small production line of three small bowls that contain, in order, the seasoned flour, the whisked egg mix and finally the breadcrumbs. Dredge each prawn in the flour, shaking off any excess, then dip it in the egg mix and shake off any drips, and lastly coat in breadcrumbs. Set aside at room temperature, not in the fridge.

Heat the oil in a very large saucepan to 190°C (or until a cube of bread dropped in the oil turns golden brown in less than a minute). Once the oil is hot enough, fry the prawns on all sides till golden brown, about 2 minutes. Lift out and drain on kitchen paper.

Cut the brioche buns in half and put a good dollop of the dressing onto the insides of each piece. Lay a bed of shredded gem on the bottom of each and fill with three prawns per slider. Skewer and serve.

Chipotle Cheeseburger

We resisted putting a burger on the menu at SPUNTINO for a long time. Partly, we were motivated by protectiveness towards our sliders – we did not want to risk them being dismissed as 'small burgers'. But our regulars ground us down.

So we started making a burger, but only on request. In other words, it didn't appear on the menu, but we would serve it if asked. This became the worst-kept secret in Soho. After a few months, we bowed to the inevitable.

For six burgers:
125g Mayonnaise – see page 152
25g chipotle chilli paste
900g finely ground beef mince
Flaky sea salt and black pepper
Pinch of garlic powder
Olive oil
6 slices of Gruyère
6 Brioche Buns, burger size – see page 160
Sliced pickled jalapeños

Put the mayonnaise, chipotle paste and a splash of cold water into a bowl and mix together well. Set aside.

Place the beef in a large mixing bowl with a few good pinches of sea salt, a twist of black pepper and the garlic powder. Mix thoroughly but gently, making sure you don't overwork the mince; the looser the mix the more juicy the burger will be. Gently roll into six 150g balls and set aside.

Heat a griddle pan with a little oil and at the same time, turn on the grill. Griddle pans leave lovely seared grill lines on the meat but if you haven't got one, you could use a heavy-based frying pan instead.

Griddle or fry each patty for 4–5 minutes on each side and then transfer to the grill. Place a slice of Gruyère on top of each and grill till the cheese has melted.

Split the brioche buns, smear chipotle mayonnaise on each side, place a burger on each and top with jalapeños.

Yonah Schimmel's Knish Bakery

Lower East Side, Chinatown, TriBeCa

About 3 miles
1 hour walking plus pit stops
Best time of day: noon
Subway: Second Avenue. F and M trains

Warning: Opening times change and places come and go. Please check availability before heading to any specific eating place.

As you emerge blinking from the Second Avenue subway station you are confronted by a street with a distinct lack of charm – Houston Street. It's one of the main downtown east/west arteries and it rumbles all day long with traffic hurtling from the East River to the Hudson and vice versa.

This is the north-western edge of the Lower East Side, once a densely packed, working-class, immigrant neighbourhood, and famously the Jewish quarter from the mid-nineteenth century well into the twentieth. Some parts remain largely unchanged; a small number of the tiny residential buildings on Orchard Street have been preserved beautifully by the Tenement Museum. But the area has undergone dramatic gentrification in the past few decades and these days it is an undeniably vibrant and fashionable neighbourhood and cultural hub, packed with boutiques, restaurants, bars and hotels. Is this a good thing? The jury is still out.

But let's start at ugly old Houston.

Looking rather tired and pretty much unchanged since 1910, you will find Yonah Schimmel's Knish Bakery on the south side of the street, opposite the subway exit (137 E. Houston St). It sells one thing and one thing only, and it is an essential New York experience. A knish is a large, stodgy potato and buckwheat cake and the ones on offer here are made to the original recipe first baked in 1890, when the business operated from a cart. To this day, the bakery is still run by the same family. Take a moment to read the press cuttings and captions underneath the faded photographs on the wall opposite the counter; everyone from Woody Allen to Jamie Oliver has been in for nosh, and no city mayor in the last 50 years has been elected to office without having their photograph taken while munching on one of Yonah's knishes.

Katz's Deli

Turn right out of the bakery and head east for a couple of blocks and you'll find Russ & Daughters (179 E. Houston St), our next pit-stop. This family-run deli is famous for its caviar, cured and smoked fish, bagels and various 'appetizers', but it is the interior that thrills me most. It's beautiful; a real feast for the eyes, with every square inch of shelf space groaning under packets, tins, jars and boxes. I have never known the place not heaving with customers. If you have the appetite, I'd recommend a Fancy Delancey – smoked tuna with horseradish dill cream cheese and flying fish roe on a bagel.

Now, turn right out of Russ & Daughters, continue east for a block and you'll come to one of the most famous restaurants in the world, Katz's Deli (205 E. Houston St). The iconic sign juts out high into the sky and the queues often snake down Ludlow Street. There will almost certainly be hordes of tourists with their noses pressed against the windows watching the army of slicers making thousands of salt beef (UK) or corned beef (US) sandwiches daily. It really is a sight to behold.

Once inside, the frenetic sense of industry is palpable. There is an archaic voucher system of entry – a rather involved way of ensuring that no-one does a runner – a vast counter of meats, and a restaurant space the size of a car-park. It's a wonderfully buzzy place with classic, old-school brusque service of the 'Whaddya want?' variety. Katz's is probably best remembered as the setting for Meg Ryan's faked orgasm in *When Harry Met Sally* and there is a big sign above the table where she and Billy Crystal sat: 'I'll have what she's having.'

To continue the walk, turn right onto Ludlow and, two blocks south, turn left onto Rivington, where you will find Economy Candy (108 Rivington St) on the left-hand side. This Aladdin's Cave of a sweet shop is guaranteed to make you grin, and if it doesn't transport you immediately to your childhood, well, I mourn the passing of your inner child.

Russ & Daughters

Economy Candy

Lower East Side, Chinatown, TriBeCa

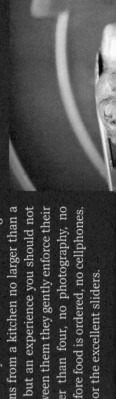

Essex Street Market

It is a joyful place, bursting at the seams with humour and love, not to mention sugar. I have never left Economy Candy empty-handed.

Ready for a drink? You're in for a treat. Carry on along Rivington to the corner of Norfolk Street. We're going to Schiller's Liquor Bar (131 Rivington St). This most beautiful of watering holes is the creation of one of my New York food heroes, Keith McNally, whose restaurants have transformed downtown dining over the past 25 years. The cocktails are excellent (go on, treat yourself, you're on vacation) but the interior is the star of the show. McNally manages to pull off an atmosphere of authentic, visceral decrepitude that has been much copied but never equalled. His perennially popular SoHo brasserie, Balthazar, is better known but, in my opinion, Schiller's Liquor Bar is the most satisfying of his places.

Leaving Schiller's, retrace your steps along Rivington and take the first left into Essex Street, where you'll be confronted by the rather brutal red-brick architecture of Essex Street Market. Don't be deterred. Once inside you can easily while away half an hour walking around the stalls: I don't know where else you can get Nordic delicacies, American cheeses, religious artefacts, budget underwear and a haircut all under one roof.

But we are here specifically to pay homage to another of my heroes, Kenny Shopsin, one of the city's true originals. An opinionated chef and restaurateur whose empire is now crammed into four hundred square feet of market space, he operates a thirty-cover restaurant serving a menu of more than two hundred items from a kitchen no larger than a closet. It is as eccentric as it sounds but an experience you should not miss. His son Zack helps out and between them they gently enforce their 'rules' – no sharing, no tables larger than four, no photography, no blogging or taking notes, no drinks before food is ordered, no cellphones. I always order Blisters On My Sisters or the excellent sliders.

Schiller's Liquor Bar

Dahing Seafood

Nom Wah Tea Parlor

You'll need to walk off some calories, so stroll south along Essex Street for four blocks until you get to Canal Street, then turn right and continue several blocks until you hit Bowery. You are now at one of the busiest junctions downtown, where traffic from five directions funnels towards the Manhattan Bridge. It always amazes me how the character of the city changes so dramatically within just a few streets. Now you will feel the unique energy of Chinatown. Take some time to mooch around Canal Street and its tributaries. It's a real eye-opener. Mott Street, two blocks west of the Bowery, is the epicentre of the neighbourhood.

I have seen some remarkable things on my ambles through Chinatown, including bathtubs full of live frogs at Dahing Seafood (127 Mott St), immense carps and catfish efficiently dispatched with a truncheon, and terrifying snow crabs escaping across the sidewalk at the K L Seafood Corp (141 Mott St). When you've had enough, return to your starting point at Bowery and Canal, head south three blocks and turn right into Doyers Street. As the road turns you will see the Nom Wah Tea Parlor (13 Doyers St). Here is the quintessential Chinatown experience, with so much charm that you really don't need to look anywhere else for your dim-sum fix.

If you've had something to eat at each of these downtown food landmarks then you've earned a drink. Head back to Canal Street. Savour the long walk west taking in the street traders, the souvenir shops flogging plastic Statues of Liberty and NYPD baseball caps and the dodgy characters in hoodies selling fake Rolexes. On the right you'll see Canal Lighting & Parts (313 Canal St). This is where I found the carbon filament lightbulbs that became such a feature at SPUNTINO. Turn left onto West Broadway and at the next corner you'll see the Nancy Whiskey Pub (1 Lispenard St). This is your final destination.

It's a genuine, spit and sawdust pub that fills up in the evenings with off-duty cops from the nearby precinct and firefighters from the local station. I strongly recommend a cold beer and a game of shuffleboard.

Nancy Whiskey Pub

Fish Plates

As you navigate its concrete canyons and skyscrapers, it is very easy to forget that Manhattan is an island. Flanked to the north, east and west by rivers, and to the south by the Atlantic Ocean, it is no surprise that a city surrounded by water should have such a close relationship with fish and seafood.

Until recently, the city's piscatorial pursuits were centred on the immense Fulton Street Fish Market at the foot of Brooklyn Bridge. This impressive building still stands, but it now houses restaurants and fancy shops. The fish market relocated to the Bronx and now handles most of New York's international fishing cargoes and local catches.

Despite the lack of a central hub, fish and seafood feature prominently and proudly on restaurant menus. Lobster, crab, shrimp and oysters crop up with thrilling regularity and, I have to confess, I can rarely resist ordering all of them. Incidentally, there are few better ways of sharpening your pre-lunch appetite than by taking a morning stroll through Chinatown – the vast displays of live crustacea and vibrantly fresh fish always do the trick for me.

Back in London at SPUNTINO, we have a healthy relationship with Billingsgate Fish Market and with a small gang of direct suppliers on the south coast. Being an island nation surrounded by sea does have its benefits. The majority of our catch comes from Sussex, Dorset, Devon and Cornwall. With this supply route, we can respond to the market and the seasons, and if you are lucky enough to have a local fishmonger I would recommend getting to know him. He will be able to tell you what's particularly good and tip you off about what's coming in tomorrow. With many of the recipes in this section you can substitute the main fishy character with an understudy, if the first choice is not available.

Soho Clam Chowder

I enjoy a good food fight, just like the next fellow, and there is sport to be had listening to food bores argue over the 'correct' versions of many a well-known dish. I've seen near fisticuffs over the right way to make a Caesar salad and I've heard raised voices about the authentic recipe for steak tartare.

Chowder is also one of those dishes that gets danders up. Are we New Englanders, rooting for chopped clams? Or do we serve it with milk and cream like Nova Scotians? Does it contain broken-up saltine crackers? Or potatoes? Or corn? Or are we Manhattanites, eschewing cream, milk and potatoes altogether in favour of tomatoes?

We could of course plead the Fifth Amendment. But that would be cowardly – so we proudly announce ours as Soho Clam Chowder.

For six to eight:
Extra virgin olive oil
2 onions, finely diced
3 garlic cloves, finely chopped
1 fennel bulb, halved, cored and finely diced
1 leek, finely diced and washed thoroughly
200g pancetta, finely diced
6 corn cobs
600ml dry white wine
2.5 litres fish stock
2kg small clams
120g butter
500ml milk
100g plain flour
Flaky sea salt and black pepper
1 bunch of chives, chopped
2 tomatoes, seeds and pith removed, finely chopped

Heat a few good glugs of olive oil in a large saucepan and gently sweat the onion, garlic, fennel, leek and pancetta. Turn a few times with a wooden spoon and sauté for 10 minutes or so until everything has just softened - you don't want the vegetables to take on any colour.

Meanwhile, remove any husks from the corn cobs and put to one side. Then stand each cob upright with the wider, flatter base on the chopping board. Take a sharp knife and run it down the sides of the cob to remove the kernels.

Now add these to the pan and continue cooking for a further 5 minutes. Then put in the wine along with the corn husks (if you have them), increase the heat to high and boil to reduce the wine by half.

Next add the fish stock and bring to the boil, then reduce to medium for a rolling boil. Skim off any scum and cook to reduce the liquid by one-third. Remove and discard the husks – they were only there to enhance the flavour.

While the stock is cooking, wash the clams. Submerge them in cold water for 5 minutes. Then gently rub them together to release the sand. Lift them out of the water and into a colander to rinse and drain well. You should store them in the fridge until you need them.

In a separate pan melt the butter on a low heat and in another pan gently heat the milk. Once the butter has melted, carefully add the flour while continuously stirring with a wooden spoon until you have a paste. Then gradually add the hot milk, ladle by ladle, incorporating thoroughly, making sure there are no lumps. Add this slowly to the pan with the corn, whisking to combine. Taste for seasoning.

Now, in yet another clean pan, heat a glug of olive oil and add the clams. Cover with a lid and steam until the clams are just starting to open, minutes only. Once you have discarded any that have not opened, tip the clams into the chowder.

Garnish the chowder with the chives and chopped tomato. Serve with crusty bread and butter.

Clams, Borlotti Beans & Wild Garlic

Borlotti beans are beautiful. The pink, purple and white pattern of the pods has been compared to Missoni fabric. And the beans are similarly stippled. How disappointing, then, that the colours fade away during the cooking process and they end up a uniform mid-brown. It's a good job they are so tasty – otherwise this drab metamorphosis would be unforgivable.

Wild garlic has a short season in Britain, usually mid-March to late-May, but it is wonderful. It is exceptionally fragrant and begs to be used when you can find it. (The tiny white flowers, if you can get them, make a good final garnish.) If your timing is slightly off, don't worry. You can pick up garlic chives at Chinese supermarkets and these work very well.

For four:
200g dried borlotti beans, soaked in cold water overnight
1 onion, halved
2 carrots, cut into large chunks
2 celery sticks, cut into large chunks
4 sprigs of rosemary
1 head of garlic, cut in half horizontally
Extra virgin olive oil
Flaky sea salt and black pepper
500g small clams, washed
1 garlic clove, finely chopped
Knob of butter
50ml dry sherry
100g wild garlic, washed and cut into 3cm strips

Drain the soaked borlotti beans and put them in a large saucepan. Add the onion, carrots, celery, rosemary, head of garlic and 75ml olive oil. Add enough water to cover generously. Place over a high heat to bring to the boil, then reduce to medium for a rolling boil and cover. After about an hour, once the beans are cooked, discard the vegetables and herbs, transfer the beans to a clean container and season well with flaky sea salt and black pepper. Reserve the cooking liquid.

Heat a good glug of olive oil in a lidded saucepan and when it's hot, throw in the clams. Cover and keep the pan over a high heat, shaking the clams around a few times. They will start to open within a few minutes. Once they do, and you have discarded any that did not open, add the beans, about 100ml of the bean cooking liquid, the chopped garlic clove, the butter and the sherry. Bring to the boil and simmer for a minute or two. Add the wild garlic strips and stir well.

Transfer the bean and clam mixture to warmed bowls. Drizzle with a little olive oil.

Mussels, Saffron & Agretti

Agretti, or saltwort, as it is known by Anglophones, is a
succulent vegetable with a really pleasing bite. It grows in
coastal areas, often right up against the shoreline, and is so
resilient and salt-tolerant that it can even be irrigated with
seawater. Its long, plump fronds are about the same thickness
as spaghetti (with which it partners brilliantly, incidentally).

You'll find agretti at farmers' markets and greengrocers'
in spring. Samphire is a decent substitute.

For four:
Extra virgin olive oil
5 shallots, thinly sliced
2 garlic cloves, finely chopped
Flaky sea salt and black pepper
100ml white wine
Good pinch of saffron strands
250ml fish stock
400ml double cream
500g mussels, washed and beards removed (discard any that
    do not close when tapped)
150g agretti
1 lemon, quartered

Place a large saucepan over a low heat with a good glug of olive oil.
Add the shallots, garlic, a pinch of salt and a twist of pepper. Sweat
until the shallots are soft but have not taken on any colour. Add the
wine and saffron, increase the heat to high and boil to reduce the liquid
by half. Add the fish stock and bring back to the boil, then reduce the
heat for a rolling boil. Using a small ladle, remove any scum that forms
on top. Reduce the liquid by half, then add the cream. Bring it back
to the boil and then remove from the stove.

Put the mussels in a large lidded pan with a glug of olive oil. Place
over a high heat with the lid in place and cook for 2 or 3 minutes,
shaking occasionally, until the mussels start to open. Discard any
that do not open.

Remove the lid and add the agretti and the saffron sauce. Bring back
to the boil. Serve immediately in deep bowls with a lemon wedge and
a hunk or two of crusty bread.

Cuttlefish, Butter Beans & Ink

I feel sorry for cuttlefish, the ugly cephalopod cousin of sleek squid. Always in the shadows, often misunderstood, sometimes thrown back in the sea by fishermen too. But these bruisers impart a startling taste of the sea and their unashamed inky blackness hints at the darkness of the deep.

The gremolata here is not a garnish, but provides an essential zing. Gremolata is very useful in brightening dishes that might otherwise be too rich. I like to use it on roast pork and it is a vital finishing touch for a classic osso buco.

For eight:
Extra virgin olive oil
1 onion, finely diced
1 leek, finely sliced
4 celery sticks, finely sliced
1 fennel bulb, halved, cored and thinly sliced
2 garlic cloves, finely chopped
Flaky sea salt and black pepper
1 teaspoon chilli flakes
500ml dry white wine
2 x 400g tins chopped tomatoes
2 x 4g sachets of cuttlefish (or squid) ink
1kg cuttlefish, cleaned and cut into 3cm pieces
100ml lemon juice
2 x 400g tins butter beans, drained and rinsed

For the gremolata:
Small handful of parsley leaves, finely chopped
Finely grated zest of 1 lemon
1 garlic clove, finely chopped

Heat a good few glugs of olive oil in a large saucepan and add the onion, leek, celery, fennel and garlic. Season with a pinch of salt, a twist of black pepper and the chilli flakes, and sweat on a low heat for 12-15 minutes. Once the vegetables are soft, add the white wine and cook for 5 minutes over a high heat. Add the tinned tomatoes and squid ink, bring to the boil, reduce the heat and simmer for 20 minutes, uncovered.

Meanwhile put a frying pan on the stove and add a good glug of olive oil. When the pan is hot, gently sauté the cuttlefish pieces on both sides. Once it has taken a little colour, add the cuttlefish to the tomato and ink sauce and leave to simmer for a further 20 minutes.

Transfer everything to a casserole dish, sprinkle over the lemon juice and cover with the lid or with foil. Put the dish into the oven preheated to 150°C/Gas 2, and cook for 3 hours. When you remove the stew from the oven, make sure the cuttlefish is soft. (If not, cook for a little longer.) Allow it to cool.

To make the gremolata, simply mix the chopped parsley, grated lemon zest and chopped garlic together in a bowl. Set aside.

Add the butter beans to the cuttlefish and gently heat through. Serve on warmed plates and scatter the gremolata over the top.

Calamari, Chickpeas & Squid Ink

Whether dried or pre-cooked in a tin, chickpeas are an incredibly useful store-cupboard staple. They add earthiness, and sometimes a smoky quality, to a variety of dishes, and work particularly well accompanied by a bold flavour such as bacon, anchovies or, in this instance, squid and ink. I've gone old-school here with the chickpeas – cooking them from scratch makes for a tastier pulse.

For four:
200g dried chickpeas, soaked in cold water overnight
1 onion, halved
2 carrots, cut into large chunks
2 celery sticks, cut into large chunks
4 sprigs of rosemary
1 head of garlic, cut in half horizontally
Extra virgin olive oil
Flaky sea salt and black pepper
500g calamari, cleaned and cut into rings, tentacles cut in half
2 garlic cloves, finely chopped
2 plum tomatoes, peeled, deseeded and finely chopped
1 bunch of spring onions, sliced thinly on an angle
150g rocket, washed
Juice of 1 lemon

For the ink dressing:
Extra virgin olive oil
2 brown anchovies, chopped
1 garlic clove, finely chopped
¼ teaspoon chilli flakes
100ml red wine
2 x 4g sachets of squid ink
2 tablespoons tomato passata
1 tablespoon white wine vinegar
Juice of ¼ lemon

Having soaked the chickpeas overnight, drain them and rinse well. Transfer them to a saucepan and cover generously with cold water. Add the onion, carrots, celery, rosemary and garlic with 75ml of olive oil. Place over a high heat, bring to the boil and then reduce to a rolling boil. Cover with a lid and cook for an hour.

Once the chickpeas are cooked, discard the vegetables and herbs, but keep the cooking liquid and set it aside. Transfer the chickpeas to a clean container and season well with flaky sea salt and ground black pepper.

For the ink dressing, place a pan over a high heat and add a glug of olive oil. Once it is smoking hot, add the anchovies so that they shatter in the hot oil. Add the garlic and chilli flakes and stir, then add the red wine and squid ink and bring to the boil. Reduce to medium for a rolling boil. Reduce the liquid by half then add the passata. Bring back up to the boil and take off the heat immediately to cool down.

Once the dressing has cooled, whisk in the vinegar and lemon juice. Using a stick blender (or an energetic whisk) slowly add 2 tablespoons of olive oil so that it emulsifies. Season with flaky sea salt and black pepper.

Place a large frying pan over a high heat and add a glug of olive oil. When smoking hot, throw in half the calamari, and cook until coloured on all sides. Transfer to a plate and repeat with the remaining calamari, adding a good pinch of salt, a twist of pepper and the chopped garlic to the pan too. Return the first batch of squid to the pan. Now add the chickpeas with a splash of the cooking liquid and toss to combine.

Remove from the heat and add the chopped tomatoes, the sliced spring onions, the rocket and the lemon juice. Mix well and distribute onto four plates, with the reheated squid ink dressing drizzled over the top.

Soft-shell Crab & Tabasco Mayonnaise

Soft-shell crabs are a thrilling addition to any menu. I wonder how many diners imagine that these unfortunate crustaceans have been cursed with inadequate armour for the dogfish-eat-dogfish world of the ocean bed. The mundane truth, of course, is that soft-shell crabs have been caught at the juvenile transition between one hard shell, recently cast off, and the next size up. It is a temporary state; the window of opportunity is small. Ask your fishmonger in advance if he can get hold of soft-shell crabs – decent frozen ones are usually available all year round.

For four:
100g Italian 00 flour
20g cornflour
Flaky sea salt and black pepper
150ml fizzy water
Vegetable oil, for frying
4 soft-shell crabs

To serve:
1 fennel bulb, halved, cored and sliced thinly on a mandoline
200g Tabasco Mayonnaise – see page 152
1 lemon, quartered - optional

Put the Italian flour and the cornflour into a large bowl and mix them together. Season with a couple of good pinches of sea salt and a few twists of black pepper. Slowly add the fizzy water while mixing vigorously, using a whisk, to make a batter. Set aside.

Half fill a large pan with the vegetable oil and heat to 190°C (or until a cube of bread dropped in the oil turns golden brown in less than a minute).

Place the crabs in the batter, make sure they are fully coated, and gently drop them into the hot oil. Cook for a couple of minutes until golden brown. Remove from the hot oil and drain on kitchen paper.

Serve with the sliced fennel, a large spoonful of the Tabasco mayonnaise and a lemon wedge.

Pickled Herring, Dill & Jersey Royals

You will need to start preparing this dish a week before you can eat it, but it is well worth the effort of pickling your own herrings. There is a lovely sweetness in this pickle liquor, with none of the puckering acidity you sometimes get with supermarket-bought roll-mops. You will only need four fillets for this recipe to serve four people, but the remaining fillets can be kept in the fridge, well submerged in their liquor, for several weeks.

The short Jersey Royal season peaks in May – feel free to substitute with small new potatoes if Jerseys are not available.

For four:
500ml white wine vinegar
500g caster sugar
12 juniper berries
12 black peppercorns
5cm fresh horseradish, grated
2 carrots, thinly sliced
3 red onions, thinly sliced
5 bay leaves
1 fennel bulb, thinly sliced
8 herrings, filleted
Flaky sea salt and black pepper

For the potato salad:
8 Jersey Royals or new potatoes, about 600g
Fine salt
¼ large bunch of dill, leaves picked and roughly chopped – keep a few
    sprigs for garnish
50g capers
200g crème fraîche

First you need to pickle the herrings. In a stainless-steel pan, heat the vinegar, 200ml cold water, sugar, juniper berries, peppercorns and horseradish until the sugar is thoroughly dissolved. Remove from the heat, add the carrot, red onion, bay leaves and fennel and leave to cool to room temperature. Layer the herring fillets in a plastic container and then cover with the cooled pickling solution. Close the container and refrigerate for a week.

When ready to serve, make the potato salad first. Place the potatoes in a pan of salted water over a high heat and bring to the boil, then reduce the heat to medium. When the potatoes are cooked, after about 15 minutes, drain immediately and leave to cool. Once cool enough to handle, slice them at an angle into 1cm pieces. Place in a mixing bowl with most of the dill and capers and all of the crème fraîche.

Lift four of the herring fillets out of the pickling solution and drain well. Slice them at an angle into three. Take some of the prettier vegetables from the liquor along with a tablespoon of the pickling liquid and add these to the bowl with the potatoes. Season with a pinch of flaky sea salt and a twist of black pepper. Mix together, transfer to a plate and arrange the pickled herring fillets on top. Serve immediately, sprinkled with the remaining dill and capers.

Sardines on Toast

This sounds rather boring, doesn't it? That's because you're thinking of the bedsit staple that requires little more than a toaster and a tin-opener.

Sorry to disappoint you. Even tinned sardines are a fantastic fish, but they are superlative when fresh. They vary in size, so I recommend small to medium specimens, no more than 15cm long. Ask the fishmonger to do the dirty work of gutting and filleting them. This simple dish is a glorious light lunch on a summer's day, washed down with a chilled glass of fino.

For four:
Extra virgin olive oil
250g cherry tomatoes
Flaky sea salt and black pepper
Good pinch of caster sugar
Good pinch of chilli flakes
2 garlic cloves, 1 finely chopped, 1 halved
20ml sherry vinegar
8 sardines, filleted
Fine salt
8 slices of sourdough bread
Handful of basil leaves
1 lemon, cut into wedges

Place a large frying pan over a high heat. Add a good glug of olive oil and when it's hot put the whole cherry tomatoes into the pan. Once they have blistered all over, throw in a good pinch each of flaky salt, pepper, sugar and chilli flakes. Reduce the heat to medium and, using the back of a wooden spoon, gently press down on the tomatoes to release some of their juices. Add the chopped garlic and sherry vinegar and mix well. Take off the heat and set aside while you cook the sardines and grill the sourdough.

Place a large non-stick frying pan over a medium heat. Lightly season the sardines with fine salt. Drizzle the pan with olive oil and place the sardines in skin-side down. Once the sardines have coloured on that side, about 2–3 minutes, turn them over, fry for 30 seconds and then remove from the heat.

Simultaneously, on a preheated griddle pan, grill the sourdough on both sides then rub on one side with the remaining halved garlic clove.

Tear the basil leaves over the tomatoes. Evenly distribute the tomato/basil mix on top of the grilled sourdough and place on serving plates. Remove the sardines from the pan and place them on top of the tomatoes. Serve with a wedge of lemon to squeeze over.

Mackerel, Smoked Almonds, Radish & Mint

Not only is it a looker; mackerel has buckets of personality too. It's pumped full of super-healthy fatty acids as well as a Scrabble board of vitamins, and its flesh has a rare intensity of flavour. The treatment here adds a layer of freshness that cuts through the salty tang of the fish.

Smoked almonds are a little tricky to find, but I have seen them in good supermarkets. They are great to use when you want a Moorish inflection to your dishes, and they work a treat with mackerel.

For four:
Extra virgin olive oil
40g smoked almonds
12 breakfast radishes
Small handful of parsley leaves, chopped
Small handful of mint leaves, chopped
1 shallot, finely diced
6 tablespoons Vinaigrette – see page 147
Flaky sea salt and black pepper
4 mackerel, filleted
Juice of ½ lemon

Heat a glug of olive oil in a frying pan and gently fry the smoked almonds until they are just starting to colour. Drain them on kitchen paper and set aside to allow them to cool.

Using a swivel-headed peeler, shave the radishes into thin slices lengthways and put them into a large mixing bowl. Add the chopped parsley and mint along with the cooled almonds and diced shallot. Add the dressing, carefully turn the ingredients over with your hand a few times and set aside.

Place a non-stick pan over a medium heat and pour in a generous glug of olive oil. Lightly season the mackerel fillets and lay them in the pan skin-side down. Once this side has some colour, turn the mackerel over and cook for a further 30 seconds. Squeeze with lemon juice and transfer onto the salad. Serve immediately.

Sea Bream, Kohlrabi & Pine Nuts

Being in the heart of Soho, SPUNTINO attracts some interesting characters. One of the most celebrated eccentrics of recent times (but sadly before my time) was the painter Francis Bacon, who used to hold court in the Colony Room, a wonderfully miserable private members' drinking den, two flights up a dingy staircase on Dean Street. Incongruously, he was extremely fond of the juice bar at Harrods.

One time, Bacon was walking through the food hall at the famous department store when he was stopped in his tracks by what turned out to be a kohlrabi. Mesmerised by this alien vegetable, he bought it, walked over to the juice bar and said, 'Juice that, Ducky!'

I have yet to try its juice, but in thin raw slivers, with moist sea bream, tarragon and chilli, kohlrabi is delicious. The dish benefits greatly from the accompaniment of a sunny day and an icy glass of Sauvignon Blanc.

For four:
Small handful of tarragon leaves
Juice of 2 lemons
1 garlic clove, finely diced
Extra virgin olive oil
80g Mayonnaise – see page 152
1 kohlrabi
Flaky sea salt
50g pine nuts, toasted – see instructions on page 119
1 long red chilli, deseeded and finely diced
4 sea bream fillets
Fine salt

Put three-quarters of the tarragon in a blender with a third of the lemon juice, the garlic, 1 tablespoon of olive oil and the mayonnaise. Blend until the ingredients are well combined, and set aside.

Peel and cut the kohlrabi in half and slice into very thin semi-circles. Place in a bowl, add another third of the lemon juice and sprinkle over a few large pinches of sea salt. Give it a good stir and set aside.

After half an hour, drain the kohlrabi and transfer to a clean mixing bowl. Add the pine nuts, chilli and the remaining tarragon leaves, torn, and combine well.

Place a frying pan over a medium heat and add a glug of olive oil. Put the sea bream in the pan skin-side down, and season with fine salt. Once it has some colour, after about 3–4 minutes, turn over and cook for a further 30 seconds. Remove from the heat and sprinkle on the remaining lemon juice. (You may need to cook the fish in batches, depending on the size of your pan.)

Arrange the sea bream, tarragon mayonnaise and salad on four plates and serve.

Red Gurnard, Samphire, Cucumber & Borage

Gurnard is a fish that is having its day. It's an odd-looking beast, almost prehistoric in appearance, with an angular head, goggly eyes, flappy fins and a tapered body – not to mention a shocking colour. Oh, and its firm, white flesh responds with aplomb to pan frying.

Borage grows wild in the British Isles and its distinctive star-shaped blue flowers have a light, cucumbery flavour. If you can't find borage growing wild, you can sometimes get a punnet as a special order from talented greengrocers.

This simple preparation makes for a lovely, light lunch. I particularly enjoy the juxtaposition of samphire and cucumber – the merging of sea and fresh water.

For four:
½ cucumber
1 teaspoon caster sugar
Fine salt
100g samphire, washed and drained
Juice of 1 lemon
50g crème fraîche
Extra virgin olive oil
4 red gurnard fillets
Small handful of borage flowers
1 teaspoon red peppercorns, crushed

With a very sharp knife, slice the cucumber into thin discs and put them in a bowl with the sugar and a good pinch of fine salt. Set aside for half an hour.

Add the samphire, half the lemon juice and the crème fraîche to the cucumber.

Preheat the oven to 180°C/Gas 4. Place a large non-stick frying pan with an ovenproof handle over a medium heat and add a glug of olive oil. Gently place the gurnard fillets in the pan, skin-side down. Leave for a couple of minutes to get some colour on the skin and then transfer to the oven for a few more minutes until just cooked through. Sprinkle the remaining lemon juice over the fillets.

Mix the salad ingredients thoroughly and divide between four plates. Top with a gurnard fillet. Garnish with the borage flowers and red peppercorns, drizzle on a little olive oil, and serve.

Sea Bass, Fennel & Olives

This dish has a definite Greek accent. I used to take my
summer break in a small fishing village in northern Kefalonia.
Sea bass and bream would come in on rickety fishing boats
every morning and be on the barbecue by lunchtime.
Kalamata olives were always on hand.

   This recipe involves a little more art, but with delicious
rewards. I love the addition of rosemary, so abundant around
the Mediterranean, but normally associated with meat,
while the fennel lends a subtle aniseed undercurrent.

For four:
Extra virgin olive oil
1 red onion, sliced
3 garlic cloves, finely chopped
Small handful of rosemary leaves
½ teaspoon chilli flakes
100ml white wine
1 tablespoon capers
8 plum tomatoes, washed and quartered
50g Kalamata olives, pitted and sliced in half lengthways
2 small fennel bulbs, sliced
4 sea bass fillets, scaled (ask the fishmonger)
Flaky sea salt and black pepper
Juice of 1 lemon

Place a saucepan over a low heat with a glug of olive oil and gently
sweat the red onion, along with the garlic, rosemary and chilli flakes –
10 minutes should do it – until they are soft and glossy. Add the wine,
turn the heat up a little, and reduce the liquid by half. Add the capers,
tomatoes and olives, and mix through.

Preheat the oven to 160°C/Gas 3. Put a frying pan on the stove over
a medium heat with a glug of olive oil. Place the fennel slices into it
and colour well on both sides. Transfer to a roasting tray and pour the
tomato mix over. Cover with foil and cook in the preheated oven for
30 minutes. Remove. Turn the oven up to 180°C/Gas 4.

Place a large, heavy-based frying pan with an ovenproof handle over
a medium heat. Brush both sides of the sea bass fillets generously with
olive oil and season well with salt and pepper. Lay the fish in the pan
skin-side down and, once the skin is crisp, turn over and cook in the
oven for 2 minutes. Remove and sprinkle over the lemon juice.

Transfer the fennel and tomato mix onto four plates, and place the
sea bass fillets on top. Serve immediately.

Sand Sole, Capers & Brown Butter

Sand soles are similar in flavour to Dover soles but around
a third of the price, kilo for kilo. They are a diminutive fish,
too small to fillet, a perfect single portion size. This traditional
treatment with capers and brown butter is ideal.

Like Dover soles, sand soles are not at their best straight
off the boat – they eat better after two to three days.

For four:
100g day-old sourdough bread
Extra virgin olive oil
Flaky sea salt and black pepper
2 garlic cloves, 1 crushed, 1 finely chopped
4 small sand (or lemon) soles, around 200g each
Fine salt
4 bay leaves
150g butter
120g capers
Small handful of parsley leaves, finely chopped

Preheat the oven to 180°C/Gas 4. Tear the bread into small pieces and
put them into a large bowl. Mix in a good glug of olive oil, a good pinch
of sea salt and the crushed garlic. Turn a few times with your hands
and then transfer to a baking tray. Roast in the preheated oven for
10–12 minutes. Take out and set aside.

Score the skin of each fish on the diagonal, making two or three
incisions. Lightly brush the fish with olive oil and then season with fine
salt. Place on a clean baking tray with the bay leaves scattered over the
top and cook in the oven for 8–12 minutes.

Meanwhile, heat the butter in a frying pan over a medium heat until
it starts to turn brown. Add the capers with a little splash of the caper
juice from the jar, the chopped garlic, the croutons, a pinch of sea salt
and a twist of black pepper. Finally stir through the chopped parsley.

Once the fish has come out of the oven, carefully transfer onto four
plates and spoon over the brown butter mix.

Lower East Side,
Chinatown, TriBeCa

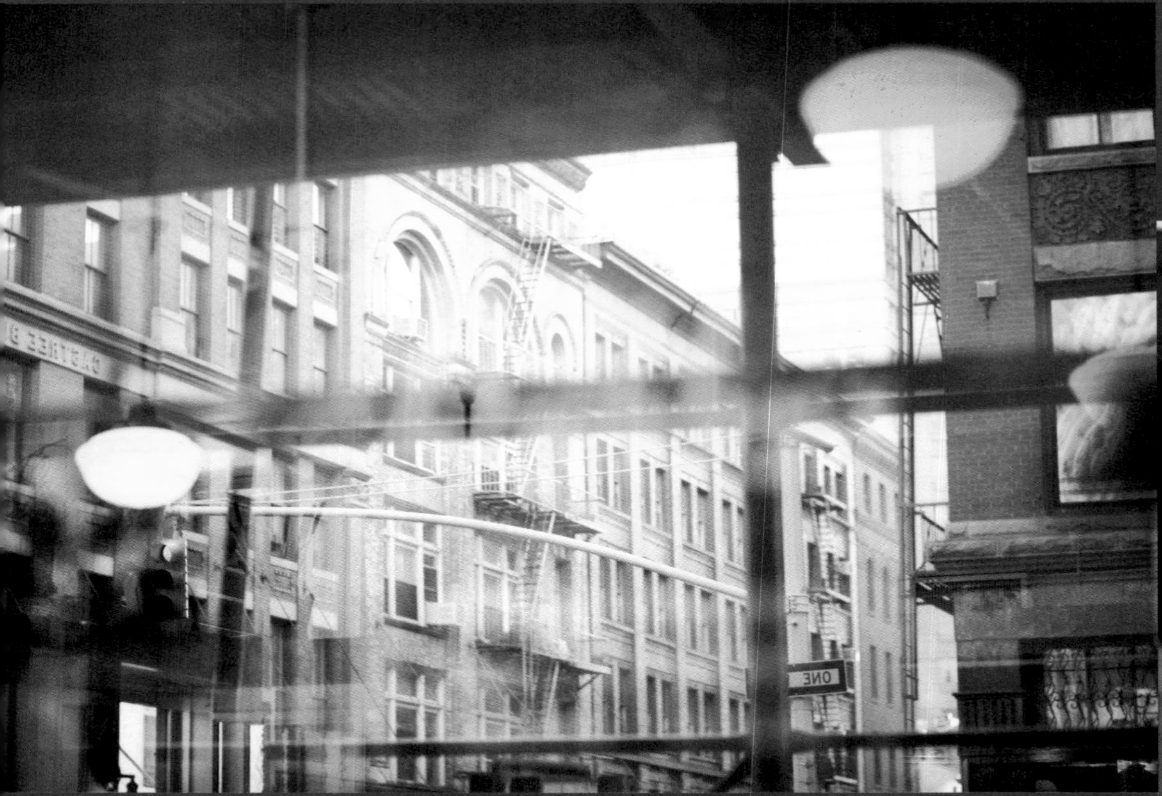

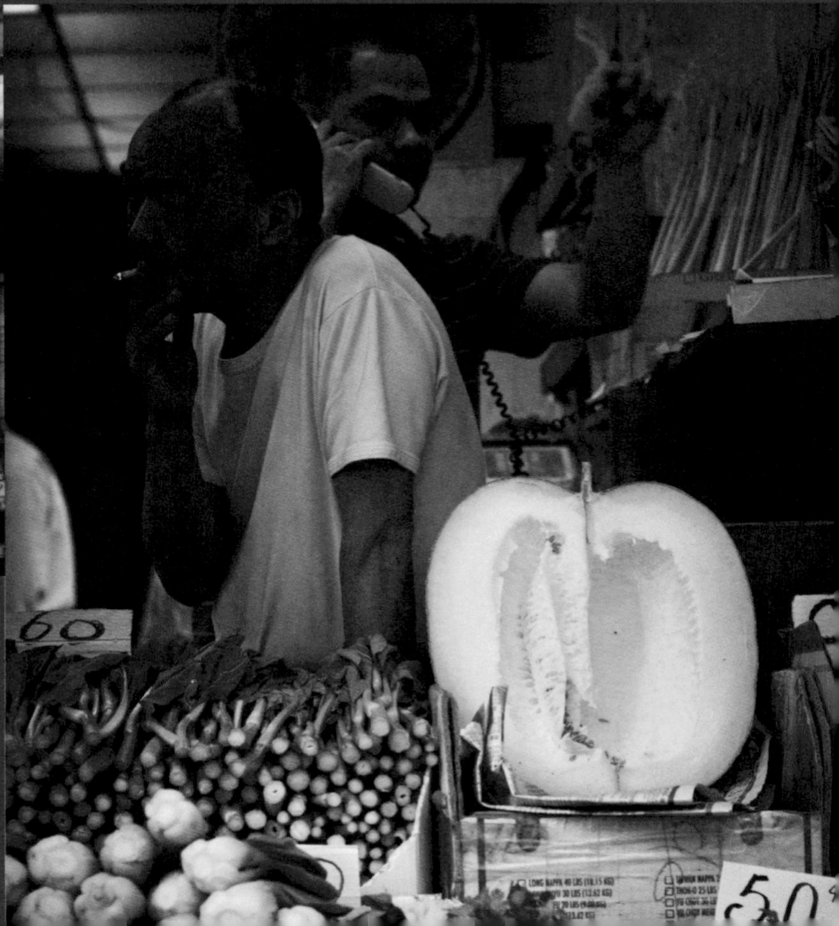

Meat Plates

In New York City, one of the ironies you will notice when visiting the Meatpacking District is that you don't see much meat packing going on. Throughout the eighteenth and nineteenth centuries the area thrived; there were more than two hundred and fifty slaughterhouses and meat processing plants between W. 14th and Gansevoort Street, the Hudson River and Hudson Street. But changes to freight routes in the city and the marching success of the supermarkets meant that from the 1970s onwards, the district's meaty credentials dwindled and it began a steady decline. Its fate was sealed when the highline trains stopped running in the 1980s. These days there's only a smattering of meat businesses left, the neighbourhood having succumbed to designer boutiques, swanky hotels and, actually, some pretty decent restaurants too.

Smithfield Meat Market in London is putting up a better fight. There is still a great deal of activity in the abattoirs and on the trading floors of the 20-acre site. Wholesale meat changes hands in vast volumes from 3am every weekday and if you ever get a chance to visit, it's a memorable experience – an absolute theatre of flesh.

But despite New York's lack of a serious meat market and perhaps in part because of Smithfield's success in London, carnivores in both cities are having their day. Meat is in. I can't remember a time when restaurant menus were as dominated by steaks, burgers, cutlets, chops and ribs as they are of late. The re-emergence of unashamedly bloodthirsty eating or what is often referred to as 'dude food' is a fashion, for sure, but it is one that shows no signs of abating.

SPUNTINO's menu celebrates meat too, but in an understated way, quite often with dishes that balance two or three elements without relying solely on the flesh. You won't find pumped-up macho steaks, I'm afraid, but you should find enough to satisfy the carnivore in you.

Fried Chicken Wings

Fried chicken is one of those very satisfying combinations of protein, fat and salt. The wing is the cheapest cut of the bird, of course, but despite its humility there is something immensely pleasurable about chewing morsels of meat from those little bones. This recipe requires some preparation, since the wings are marinated – you will find that the flavours develop the longer you leave them. And although the ingredient list for the flour mix reads like a witch's spell, each constituent is necessary for the sorcery to work.

For six (about two wings each):
1kg free-range chicken wings
1 litre vegetable oil, for deep frying

For the marinade:
1 x 284ml pot of buttermilk
½ teaspoon cayenne
1 teaspoon Chinese five spice
1 teaspoon Tabasco sauce
1 tablespoon runny honey
1 teaspoon fine salt
1 teaspoon black pepper
Flaky sea salt

For the flour:
250g plain flour
4 teaspoons paprika
2 teaspoons chilli powder
2 teaspoons garlic powder
2 teaspoons onion powder
2 teaspoons Chinese five spice
2 teaspoons cayenne
2 teaspoons celery seeds, ground
1 teaspoon fine salt
1 teaspoon black pepper

Thoroughly mix together all the marinade ingredients. Submerge the chicken wings in the mix, cover well and refrigerate. Leave for at least 6 hours before frying, but remove them from the fridge about an hour before you intend to start cooking. When you are ready, take a large bowl and combine the ingredients for the flour mixture.

Heat the vegetable oil in a medium pan to 190°C (or until a cube of bread dropped in the oil turns golden brown in less than a minute). At the same time, preheat the oven to 180°C/Gas 4.

Now, lift the chicken wings out of the marinade and transfer in batches to the flour mix. Generously dredge with the flour and then deep fry the wings for 2–3 minutes, placing each golden-brown batch on a large baking tray.

Once you have fried all the chicken, place the tray in the preheated oven and cook for a further 10–12 minutes, or until cooked through. Remove, drain briefly on kitchen paper, sprinkle with flaky sea salt, and serve hot.

Cornflake Chicken

My earliest cooking memory is making chocolate cornflake cakes with my grandmother in the 1970s. It wasn't a sophisticated dish (cornflakes, chocolate, butter, syrup) and her kitchen in London's East End was really no more than a Formica and linoleum pantry but, if I'm honest, it was at that moment that I got hooked on food.

I'm particularly fond of this recipe and quite sentimental about its use of cornflakes. They are a nostalgic reminder of my childhood, but they also provide a fantastic layer of crunch.

For four as a snack:
50g caster sugar
Fine salt and black pepper
4 skinless chicken thighs, deboned
125g cornflakes, lightly crushed
4-5 sprigs of thyme, leaves picked and chopped
3 medium eggs
Paprika
Curry powder
1 teaspoon Dijon mustard
100g plain flour
500ml vegetable oil, for deep frying

To serve:
200g 'Slaw – see page 126

Dissolve the sugar and 30g of the fine salt in 500ml cold water to make a brine, and then submerge the chicken thighs in this for 2 hours in the fridge.

In a large bowl, mix the crushed cornflakes with the chopped thyme. In a separate bowl, beat the eggs and add a pinch of paprika, a good pinch of curry powder and the mustard. Mix well. Place the flour in a third bowl, and season with fine salt and black pepper.

Remove the chicken thighs from the brine and pat dry with kitchen paper. Cut the thighs into long strips, about 1.5-2cm thick, and dredge them in the seasoned flour. Shake off any excess and dip each piece into the egg mix. Now roll in the crushed cornflakes and thyme.

Heat the vegetable oil in a medium pan to 190°C (or until a cube of bread dropped in the oil turns golden brown in less than a minute). Now fry the chicken in batches, until golden and fully cooked, about 3-4 minutes. Lift out and drain briefly on kitchen paper. Serve with a generous dollop of the 'slaw.

Spicy Sausage, Lentils & Radicchio

SPUNTINO is fortunate to have two excellent Italian delis within a 30-second walk, I Camisa on Old Compton Street and Lina Stores on Brewer Street. The former is renowned for its fabulous meats and cheeses, the latter for its superb fresh pasta and pastries. We use I Camisa's pork, fennel and garlic sausages for this recipe, but any similar sausage will do fine.

For four:
6 Italian pork, fennel and garlic sausages
250g dried Castelluccio (or Puy) lentils
1 large carrot, roughly chopped
4 celery sticks, roughly chopped
4 fennel tips from a fennel bulb (tops and fronds)
3 garlic cloves
6 sprigs of rosemary, leaves picked
Extra virgin olive oil
1 onion, finely diced
1 teaspoon chilli flakes
2 teaspoons fennel seeds, dry roasted - see page 68 - and ground
Flaky sea salt and black pepper
1 tablespoon Dijon mustard
1 head of radicchio, cut into 2cm strips
Small handful of flat parsley leaves, roughly chopped

Preheat the oven to 180°C/Gas 4. Prick the sausages and place them on a baking sheet. Roast for 20 minutes, turning once and basting them in their own juices to prevent burning or sticking. Allow them to cool slightly, then use a very sharp knife to slice at an angle into 1cm pieces. Set aside.

Meanwhile, place the lentils in a colander and wash them well, looking out for any little stones you may need to remove. Put them in a large saucepan and cover with cold water. Bring to the boil and leave bubbling for 30 seconds, then remove from the heat. Drain in the colander and set aside.

Put the carrot, celery, fennel tips, garlic and rosemary into a food processor and blend till the vegetables are finely diced. Alternatively, you could dice the vegetables with a sharp knife and finely chop the garlic and rosemary.

Now place a large saucepan over a low heat and warm a few glugs of olive oil. Gently sauté the onion for 10 minutes until glossy and translucent, then add the blended vegetables along with the chilli flakes and fennel seeds. Sweat everything for 12–15 minutes until shiny and soft.

Add the lentils and just enough cold water to cover the lot, and increase the heat to medium. Gently cook for 20–30 minutes or until the lentils are al dente. Drain.

Season the lentils while hot with salt and pepper to taste. Add the Dijon mustard and the sliced sausages and mix thoroughly, then just before serving quickly fold through the radicchio and parsley. Serve immediately.

Braised Chicory & Speck

Speck is an exceptionally tasty pork-thigh prosciutto from
Alto Adige in northern Italy. It is noticeably leaner and less
salty than its counterparts from other regions. This is because
the salting process in fact involves seasoning with juniper,
rosemary and bay, followed by a gentle smoking. The result
is an aromatic, sweet meat. Alongside the juicy braised
chicory, this is grown-up comfort food with a bitter twist.

Please ask for your speck to be sliced very thinly at the
deli counter.

For four:
200g day-old bread
Extra virgin olive oil
Flaky sea salt and black pepper
2 garlic cloves, 1 finely chopped
4 heads of chicory
250ml vegetable stock
30ml sherry vinegar
Juice of 1 orange
1 teaspoon caster sugar
Large knob of butter
50g Dijon mustard
500g speck, very thinly sliced

Preheat the oven to 160°C/Gas 3. Cut or tear the stale bread into very
rough pieces, and place them in a large bowl. Add a good glug of olive
oil and a good pinch of salt. Smash the unchopped clove of garlic with
the side of a knife and add to the bowl. Gently massage the oil and
garlic into the bread and transfer to a baking tray. Place in the oven
and leave to bake gently for 15–20 minutes until golden brown. Remove
from the oven and when cooled, roughly chop into chunky crumbs.

Turn the oven up to 180°C/Gas 4. Cut the chicory in half lengthways
and, using the tip of a sharp knife, remove the core. Heat a few glugs
of olive oil in a heavy-based frying pan over a medium to high heat.
When the oil is hot, lay the chicory halves flat-side down in it and
colour well, till almost black. Turn the chicory over and remove the
pan from the heat.

Add the vegetable stock, sherry vinegar, orange juice, a good pinch of
salt, a twist of black pepper, the finely chopped garlic, the sugar and
butter. If your frying pan can't or won't fit into your oven, transfer the

chicory to an ovenproof dish. Cover with foil and bake in the oven for 25 minutes, until just soft. Test the middle of the chicory with a knife; there shouldn't be any give. Remove the chicory and place on a large serving platter.

Transfer the cooking liquid to a saucepan and over a high flame reduce it by half, then whisk in the Dijon mustard. Pour it over the chicory, then drape sliced speck over the top. Sprinkle with the crunchy crumbs and serve.

Ribbon Steak, Chicory & Anchovy

In Italy you will often see *tagliata di manzo* on the menu in restaurants and trattorias. Literally 'ribbons of beef', it's a familiar and traditional way of serving a steak without resorting to throwing a slab of meat on a plate. It also makes a steak feel more like a salad and, dare I say it, a little more virtuous. The anchovy dressing is a robust companion here but the result, with the addition of bitter, crunchy chicory, is a dish that you might describe, with your tongue firmly in your cheek, as turf, earth and surf.

For four:
1 head of chicory
1 shallot
70g rocket, washed
250g sirloin steak, trimmed of any excess fat
Fine salt and black pepper
Extra virgin olive oil
20ml red wine vinegar
6 tablespoons Anchovy Dressing - see page 151

Cut the chicory in half lengthways and, using the tip of a sharp knife, remove the core. Slice it at an angle into bite-sized pieces. Cut the shallot in half, remove the skin and slice very thinly. Place these ingredients into a large mixing bowl along with the washed rocket. Set aside.

Slice the steak into thin ribbons, place in a bowl, season and toss with a little olive oil. Heat a griddle pan until hot and cook the steak ribbons for 1 minute on each side, depending on thickness, or just until browned and scorched with griddle marks.

Add the red wine vinegar - this will produce a hearty hiss and a cloud of steam. Remove the meat from the heat and set aside to rest while you dress the salad.

Pour the dressing over the prepared leaves, and toss several times till everything is thoroughly coated. Divide between warm plates and top with the warm ribbons of beef.

Grilled Baby Gem Lettuce, Pancetta & Anchovy

The application of heat transforms the watery leaves of baby gem, which has a heart so dense that it takes on an almost meaty consistency when grilled. Beefed up with pancetta and anchovy this lettuce really punches above its weight.

Grana Padano is an underused cheese, in my opinion. It is often upstaged by its brasher cousin Parmigiano Reggiano, but it has a distinctive texture and a sweeter, milder flavour.

For four:
100g day-old sourdough bread
Extra virgin olive oil
Flaky sea salt
6 baby gem lettuces
12 slices of pancetta
1 shallot, finely diced
Splash of red wine vinegar
6 tablespoons Anchovy Dressing – see page 151
Small piece of Grana Padano

Preheat the oven to 180°C/Gas 4. Tear the bread into rough chunks and place in a bowl with a glug of olive oil and a pinch or two of sea salt. Using your hands, turn the bread pieces several times to make sure they are well coated with oil and then lay out on a baking tray. Bake for around 10–12 minutes until golden brown. Remove, allow to cool, then roughly chop.

Cut off and discard the bases of the lettuces, cut them in half lengthways, then in half again. Place a griddle pan over a high heat, lightly coat the lettuce quarters with olive oil, then lay them on the griddle pan, turning every 2 minutes so that they take on some colour. Meanwhile lay the pancetta slices flat on a baking tray and place in the oven for 3 minutes.

Put the cooked gem, chopped-up bread pieces and diced shallot into a large mixing bowl. Dress lightly with a glug of olive oil and a splash of red wine vinegar. Divide between four plates, laying the cooked pancetta over the top. Drizzle with the anchovy dressing, then grate the cheese over the top.

Strozzapreti &
Spicy Sausage

Strozzapreti is a type of pasta that consists of short lengths
that are twisted and curled inwards. It is particularly good
at capturing sauce. But its etymology is the tastiest part.
It means 'priest strangler'. Now, call me old-fashioned, but
I can't imagine a culinary scenario in which a member of the
clergy is murdered by manual asphyxiation, but it turns out
there are many theories as to how this pasta acquired its
name. Check them out, if you have a few spare minutes.

Good-quality spicy Italian sausages are available in most
delis and even in supermarkets. It's worth splashing out on
the more expensive ones – they tend to be firmer, meatier,
tastier and less watery.

For four:
6 spicy Italian sausages
Extra virgin olive oil
1 onion, finely sliced
1 fennel bulb, finely sliced
1 garlic clove, finely sliced
Small handful of sage, leaves picked and chopped
2 teaspoons chilli flakes
1 teaspoon fennel seeds, ground
Flaky sea salt and black pepper
125ml white wine
400g strozzapreti pasta
400ml Basic Tomato Sauce - see page 89

Preheat the oven to 180°C/Gas 4. Put the sausages on a baking tray,
prick them with a fork and drizzle with a little olive oil. Place in the
oven and cook for 20 minutes. Remove and leave to cool.

Meanwhile, put a large saucepan over a low heat and add a good glug
of olive oil, the onion, fennel, garlic, sage, chilli, fennel seeds, a large
pinch of salt and a good twist of black pepper. Sweat until the onions
are soft and translucent but not browned. Add the white wine, turn up
the heat and reduce the liquid by half.

Now, cut the sausages in half lengthways, then into thin slices across.

Place a covered pan of salted water over a high heat and bring to the boil. Add the strozzapreti and cook according to the instructions on the packet, but do test to make sure the pasta is al dente. It usually takes about 8–10 minutes. Drain well.

Meanwhile, add the sausage and the tomato sauce to the onions in the large saucepan and gently heat until the sauce starts to bubble. Now transfer the drained pasta to the sauce, mix well, remove from the heat and serve.

Ham Hock & Savoy

Ham hock, sometimes called pork knuckle, is the joint
between the pig's thigh and its ankle. It is the shank end
of the animal's leg. There's a lot of tendon and ligament in
the hock so it needs slow cooking to tenderise it and to allow
it to develop its flavour. And, my goodness, there's a lot of
flavour, as is often the case with the cheapest, least refined
cuts of meat.

Pairing meat as unctuous as this with something as
simple and hearty as Savoy cabbage is all that's needed.

For four:
2 small unsmoked ham hocks, or 1 large, weighing a total of 1.2kg
Extra virgin olive oil
2 onions, roughly chopped
2 carrots, thickly sliced
4 celery sticks, thickly sliced
1 head of garlic, cut in half horizontally
250ml white wine
50ml cider vinegar
2 litres chicken stock
8 black peppercorns
2 star anise
6 cloves
1 cinnamon stick, broken in half
½ head Savoy cabbage
Fine salt
1 shallot, finely sliced
6 tablespoons Lemon Mustard Dressing – see page 146

Preheat the oven to 180°C/Gas 4.

Put the ham hocks on a baking tray and coat with olive oil. Place in the
oven and roast for 25-30 minutes or until the hocks are coloured a little.
Remove from the oven.

Meanwhile, gently heat a few glugs of olive oil in a large saucepan and
add the onion, carrot, celery and garlic. Cover and sweat until soft and
glossy, about 15 minutes, stirring every so often. Add the white wine,
turn up the heat and reduce the liquid by half.

Add the roasted ham hocks to the saucepan along with the cider
vinegar, chicken stock, peppercorns, star anise, cloves and cinnamon.
Cover the pan with a lid, bring to the boil, then reduce the heat and
simmer for 2½ hours. The meat should yield immediately when ready

so make sure you check by pushing a bit of it away from the bone with a fork. Lift the meat out of the pan and lay it on a tray to cool a little.

Meanwhile, cut the cabbage into ribbons and blanch for 4 minutes in a pan of salted boiling water. Strain and set aside.

Now pass the cooking liquid from the hocks through a fine sieve and also set aside. You will use some in the recipe, but don't throw away the rest, as it is packed with flavour. You can freeze it and use it to make soup at a later date.

Once the meat is cool enough to handle, gently take it off the bone in large chunks, discarding any fat. Transfer this meat to a pan and add 200ml of the cooking liquid and the sliced shallot. Gently heat until just bubbling, then add the blanched cabbage and the dressing. Remove from the heat and mix gently with a wooden spoon, taking care not to break up the pieces of meat. Divide equally between four warmed plates and serve.

Oxtail, Cavolo Nero & Mash

This dish requires a little forward planning – the oxtails are marinated a day in advance – but the resulting intensity of flavour makes it all worthwhile. Braised meats such as oxtail benefit from a comforting companion like mashed potato. As you eat this dish, the meat, the juices and the mash all end up mixing with each other till you're left with a wonderful mess. What it lacks in good looks it makes up for in personality.

For four:
8 medium oxtail pieces
1 onion, roughly chopped
3 carrots, roughly chopped
3 celery sticks, roughly chopped
1 head of garlic, cut in half horizontally
Small handful of thyme
6 bay leaves
12 black peppercorns
1 bottle of red wine
1.5 litres chicken stock
Vegetable oil
200g plain flour
Fine salt and black pepper
1 head of cavolo nero, about 200g, destalked

For the mash:
1kg waxy potatoes, peeled and cut
250g unsalted butter, diced
250ml whole milk, warmed
Flaky sea salt

You will need a very large saucepan that fits in your fridge and a round plate that is just a little smaller than the saucepan. Put the oxtail into the pan with the chopped vegetables, garlic, herbs, and peppercorns. Empty the red wine into the pan too and place baking parchment on top of the ingredients. Weigh down with the plate, cover and refrigerate for 24 hours. Alternatively you could try getting everything into a very large, lidded plastic container.

Next day, remove the oxtail from the marinade. Strain the vegetables, retaining the wine only. Add the wine and chicken stock to a large saucepan and place over a medium to high heat.

Meanwhile, heat a few glugs of vegetable oil in a heavy-based frying pan. Season the flour with fine salt and black pepper. Dredge the oxtail in seasoned flour, shake off any excess and fry in batches in the hot oil until really well browned all over. Add to the large saucepan, and

submerge in the wine and stock: you may need to add a little more stock
or water if the meat isn't completely covered. Put the lid on, bring to the
boil, reduce to a low heat so that it is just bubbling, and cook for 3 hours
until the meat comes away from the bone without any resistance.

To make the mash, rinse the peeled potatoes well under cold water.
Place in a large pan of salted water, cover and bring to the boil. Reduce
the heat and simmer until tender, about 15-20 minutes. Once the
potatoes are cooked, drain and leave them to let off steam in the
colander for a few minutes. Transfer them back to the used pan and
mix in the butter, letting it melt over the potatoes. Using a masher
or a ricer, form a smooth paste with the buttery potatoes. Stir in the
warmed milk gradually - you may not need it all - and a good few
pinches of flaky salt.

Once the oxtail is cooked, remove from the pan and keep warm. To
make the sauce, transfer 4 ladlefuls of the cooking liquid to a small
pan. Boil vigorously until reduced and thickened, then strain through
a fine sieve.

Simultaneously, thickly slice the cavolo nero then blanch in a pan of
boiling water for 4 minutes and drain.

To serve, dollop some mash onto four warmed plates, then distribute
the blanched cavolo nero on top. Finally, place two oxtail pieces on
each plate, and spoon over a generous amount of the sauce.

Beef Cheek, Kale & Cauliflower

It started around the end of 2012 in New York and soon afterwards spread to London. It first infected restaurants, of course, and then inveigled itself into supermarkets, before contaminating people's homes. It is now a full-blown epidemic that shows no signs of abating. Yes, kale is back.

Its rediscovery after so many years in the vegetable doldrums is hard to explain – but I for one am rather glad. Kale crops up on the SPUNTINO menu in various incarnations, particularly amongst the salads, but here shows its rugged, macho credentials alongside meaty beef cheeks.

For six:
1kg beef cheek, sinew and silver skin removed
1 onion, roughly chopped
2 carrots, roughly chopped
2 celery sticks, roughly chopped
4 sprigs of rosemary
6 bay leaves
Zest of 1 orange
10 black peppercorns
1 bottle of red wine
250ml sweet sherry
1 litre chicken stock
Vegetable oil
100g plain flour
Fine salt and black pepper
1 large bunch of kale, about 200g

For the cauliflower purée:
100g butter
1 onion, thinly sliced
Flaky sea salt
1 large cauliflower
750ml milk

Put the meat into a large lidded plastic container and cover with the chopped vegetables, herbs, zest and peppercorns. Empty the wine into the container so that the beef is completely submerged. Cover with a lid and refrigerate for 24 hours.

The next day lift the meat out of the marinade and set aside. Strain the vegetables, keeping only the wine. Place a large pan over a medium heat and add the wine, sherry and chicken stock. Bring to the boil, then reduce to a simmer.

Meanwhile heat a few glugs of oil in a heavy-bottomed frying pan. Season the flour with fine salt and black pepper. Dredge the beef cheeks in seasoned flour, shake off any excess and fry in batches until well browned all over. Place the meat in the simmering liquid, cover and cook for 3½ hours until the meat is soft and tender. You should be able to push a fork into the flesh with no resistance.

While the meat is cooking, you should make the cauliflower purée. Melt the butter in a large saucepan and gently sauté the onion for 10 minutes or so, until soft and translucent. Add a good pinch of sea salt. Break the cauliflower into florets and add them to the saucepan along with the milk: if the cauli isn't covered, top up with more milk. Cover and cook on a low to medium heat for about 12 minutes until soft. Strain the cauliflower and put it into a blender but retain the cooking milk. Purée the soft florets, adding a little of the liquid if necessary but taking care not to make it too soupy. It should have a smooth, silky texture. Season with flaky sea salt.

Once the beef cheeks are cooked, lift them out of the liquid and keep warm. To make the sauce, transfer 5 ladlefuls of the cooking liquid to a small pan. Boil vigorously until reduced and thickened, then strain through a fine sieve. Meanwhile, cut the kale into strips and plunge into a pan of boiling water for 4 minutes.

If you have coordinated well, all the elements will be hot and ready at the same time. Using a very sharp knife, divide the beef cheeks into thick slices. Spoon the cauliflower purée onto six warmed plates, then add the blanched kale, and finally top each plate with the sliced beef cheek. Spoon over a little of the sauce and serve.

Steak Tartare

I must say, I really do enjoy the traditional preparation of steak tartare that you often see in old-school French brasseries. The trolley, the white-coated waiter, the hand-cut steak, the mixing of shallots and capers tableside. It's up there with flambéed crêpe Suzette and filleted Dover sole as one of the great spectacles of restaurant theatre.

    Our version comes with a little less drama but it still delivers a convincing performance. I like my steak tartare with lashings of Tabasco and Worcestershire sauce, but not everyone does. Best to leave those condiments on the table for personal fine-tuning.

For four:
½ ciabatta loaf
Extra virgin olive oil
500g flank steak
2 echalion (banana) shallots, finely diced
30g cocktail gherkins, finely diced
10g capers, chopped
Small handful of tarragon leaves, chopped
Flaky sea salt and ground pepper
2 tablespoons tomato ketchup
2 tablespoons Mayonnaise – see page 152
4 small egg yolks

Preheat the oven to 150°C/Gas 2. Thinly slice the ciabatta into about 16 pieces, approximately 5mm thick. Place them on a lightly oiled baking tray, and bake for approximately 15 minutes until golden brown. Set aside.

Using a very sharp knife, thinly slice the steak, place on a plate, and put into the freezer for 20–30 minutes to firm it up a little.

Meanwhile place the shallots, gherkins, capers and tarragon into a large bowl and mix well. When the meat is firm but not frozen, dice it into very small pieces using a sharp knife. Combine the chopped meat with the shallot mix, a good pinch of salt, the ketchup and the mayonnaise, turning everything over several times to mix well.

Using a 10cm mousse ring, lightly press the mixture onto each of four plates. Make a slight well in the centre of each with the back of a teaspoon and gently place the egg yolks on top. Season with a generous pinch of flaky salt and a twist of black pepper. Serve with the baked ciabatta, a bottle of Worcestershire sauce and a bottle of Tabasco.

Williamsburg Bridge

Williamsburg

Including Williamsburg Bridge:
About 4 miles
1½ hours walking plus pit stops
Subway: Essex Street (Manhattan).
J and Z trains

Excluding Williamsburg Bridge:
About 2 miles
45 minutes walking plus pit stops
Subway: Hewes Street (Brooklyn).
J and Z trains

Best time of day: Saturday afternoons

Warning: Opening times change and places come and go. Please check availability before heading to any specific eating place.

From Manhattan, exit the Essex Street subway station and head east along Delancey towards the Williamsburg Bridge. When you reach the pedestrian approach to the bridge, make sure you choose the 'on foot' lane – the cyclists and rollerbladers are relentless (and remorseless).

Built in 1903, the Williamsburg Bridge has always been in the shadow (figuratively speaking) of the beefier Brooklyn Bridge, but I feel more affinity with the Williamsburg Bridge. It is noisier, brasher and feels slightly more dangerous. This is partly because of the ugly red steel gates at either end, the rusting railings and grilles along its length and the acres of graffiti. But it also has something to do with the thrill of seeing, hearing and feeling the J train hurtle past you on its tracks running parallel to the walkway. As you come off the bridge onto terra firma you should turn right, then left, and head along Broadway to the Hewes Street Station.

From Brooklyn, Hewes Street Station is your starting point if you are not walking across the East River. Just at the bottom of the steps on the south side of Broadway you will see Moto (394 Broadway). This exquisite little café-bar-restaurant had quite an effect on me when I first visited before setting up SPUNTINO. Look closely and you might be able to spot some shared DNA.

Leaving Moto, turn left and walk along Broadway back to the bridge. I love this stretch of road where the elevated section of the J train runs above you like a noisy steel canopy. Observe the sunlight catching the motes of dust as they float down from the track when a train passes.

Carry on past the Marcy Avenue Station, making sure you take in the wonderful hat shops in the parade on the left, notably Bencraft (236 Broadway) and Krausz (234 Broadway): the latter hatter sells Homburgs and nothing else. The Hasidic Jewish community in this part of Brooklyn is a striking

Nick's Luncheonette

Moto

Marlow & Sons

The Bagel Store

reminder of New York's richness and diversity. A little further along and you will see one of my favourite Williamsburg relics, a long-disused restaurant called Nick's Luncheonette (196 Broadway) with very evocative steel letters above a faded, patinated shopfront. It has been preserved not so much in aspic as in dust and street grime for as long as I can remember. Part of me hopes it stays that way forever.

Our turning is right onto Bedford Avenue but you may want to take a quick detour by continuing one block on Broadway till you get to Marlow & Sons (81 Broadway). This grocery store with a restaurant at the back was a pioneer in the early days of Williamsburg's transformation into New York's coolest neighbourhood, and its owners have been slowly populating the local gastronomic landscape ever since. Stay for a coffee and maybe pick up a copy of their excellent self-published food magazine *Diner Journal*.

Back to Bedford and the first significant store you'll notice is The Bagel Store (349 Bedford) near the corner of S. 4th Street. Here you will find the (self-proclaimed) world's greatest bagel'. Try it and see what you think. My money is still on that smoked tuna masterpiece at Russ & Daughters (see page 181).

Head north for three and a half blocks and on the left, between Grand and S. 1st Street, you'll come to Maison Premiere (298 Bedford Ave). It is billed as an oyster and cocktail bar, but it punches well above its weight. There is a kind of time-warp effect as you enter, and you could quite easily convince yourself you've stumbled into 1920s Louisiana rather than twenty-first-century Brooklyn. The exquisitely groomed bartenders have all stepped out of the same time-machine, it seems, and they make beautiful drinks with careful precision and laid-back élan. I could easily spend hours at Maison Premiere. In fact, sometimes I have.

Turn left when you leave and walk two blocks north. You will notice an imposing municipal building on the right. This is the Metropolitan

Maison Premiere

Mast Brothers

Recreation Center (261 Bedford Ave). Now, I have a thing for slightly brutal architecture, and although that might not be your cup of tea, it is really worth taking a look inside. The place was built in 1922, the interiors were designed by the architect Henry Bacon, and it's a beauty. Herringbone-patterned, glazed terracotta tiles flank the large public swimming pool and there's a full-length steel-and-glass skylight above it that is simply stunning. If you have the time, I would certainly recommend returning another day with your swimming costume.

It's only one block north along Bedford to N. 3rd Street, where you should hang a left and walk one block west to Mast Brothers (111 N. 3rd St at Berry Street). The store of this independent but globally successful chocolate-maker backs onto a very impressive and modern factory. It is more 'sci-fi set' than 'Willy Wonka', but the important thing is that the chocolate is excellent. My favourite is their Brooklyn Blend, but don't take my word for it. Each variety on sale is also helpfully displayed in sample form, too, so you can try-before-you-buy. Don't be shy.

Retrace your steps to Bedford and then turn left. One more block takes you to the Bedford Cheese Shop (229 Bedford Ave). This is a food business that is typical of the area. It is a small shop, but stocks several hundred cheeses, all on display, and staff knowledge is encyclopaedic.

Across the street, tucked inside a curious little arcade whose storefront proclaims 'Realform Girdle Co', sits Spoonbill and Sugartown Books (218 Bedford Ave). I often lose track of time in this charming, independent bookstore. Its shelves are packed with second-hand paperbacks and specialist hardbacks with a leaning towards design, architecture, cinema, philosophy and literature.

Take a gentle stroll two blocks north until you get to N. 7th Street. Here you'll see the Bedford Avenue subway station – useful to note if you need to get the L train back to Manhattan later.

Metropolitan Recreation Center

Spoonbill and Sugartown Books

Artists and Fleas

But for now, turn left along N. 7th Street for two and a half blocks until you come to Artists and Fleas (70 N. 7th St). An indoor flea market, open weekends only, full of vintage stalls and quirky designers, Artists and Fleas is the place to while away half an hour and maybe pick up something you didn't know you needed until you saw it. Well, I always seem to anyway.

If you've timed your walk carefully, and your pit stops haven't been too long (and it's a Saturday from April to November) then you can turn left out of Artists and Fleas and head one block west to Smorgasburg (90 Kent Ave). This food market on the shores of the East River showcases almost one hundred vendors selling pretty much everything from ribs and lobsters to tacos and cheesecake. The views aren't bad either.

But if you want the ultimate glimpse of Manhattan from the edge of Brooklyn, then hold on to your hat – there's one more stop.

Walk three blocks north up Kent and one block east on N. 11th and you come to the Wythe Hotel (80 Wythe Ave). It's an unprepossessing building that sits quite comfortably next to the Brooklyn Brewery, makers of the superb, dark and malty Brooklyn Lager. The fact that it was once a textile factory does not come as a surprise, but its conversion into a 70-room hotel is slightly at odds with its surroundings. That is, until you step inside. I'll save you the superlatives. Head straight up to The Ides, the hotel's rooftop bar. The drinks are good, but the view is breathtaking. Manhattan, in all its glory, from the tip of downtown to the edge of the Upper East Side, is a sight to behold. And don't forget, you're facing west. Depending on the time of year, you could be in for one hell of a sunset.

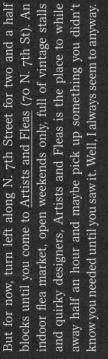

Bedford Cheese Shop

Brooklyn Brewery

Desserts

To be honest, we didn't originally plan an extensive dessert menu at SPUNTINO. Our research had focussed on the comforting savoury dishes we associated with blue-collar diners, and anyway, we expected the accompaniments of shoestring fries, grits* and the like to be more than enough to satisfy most carborific urges.

Then three things happened. The first was Rachel O'Sullivan's Brown Sugar Cheesecake (see page 246). The second was her Peanut Butter and Jelly Sandwich (see page 270). The third was her Dutch Baby (see page 257). These desserts came to us at tastings fully formed. No tweaking needed. No adjustments required. Rachel simply served up these three aces as if it were a cakewalk.

Oddly, research trips have borne meagre fruit when it comes to transporting dessert ideas across the Atlantic. I remember one trip involved eating copious quantities of cheesecake. We were on a quest for the perfect version, and tried some excellent examples, the best being those at Junior's (386 Flatbush Ave) and Eileen's (17 Cleveland Place). But those recipes didn't travel well.

Unusually for a restaurant, we tend not to ask diners if they want dessert. The choices are printed on the menu placemat that sits in front of you throughout your meal. By the time most people have demolished several shared plates, they have usually made their mind up about what comes next. They may have been eyeing a particular dessert for an hour or more, or have been casing dishes as they arrive from the kitchen. Some die-hard barflies prefer to take their dessert in liquid form. These brave souls will point to the liquor shelf behind the bar and order an Apple Pie Old Fashioned. That's hardcore.

As it happened, grits weren't something that Londoners could quite come to terms with. We put them on the menu in the very early days at SPUNTINO, but they were misunderstood at best and disliked at worst. It was a great shame, because I absolutely love them.

Brown Sugar Cheesecake & Drunken Prunes

These days we tend to downplay sugar. We are used to seeing it as an ingredient, but rarely as a principal flavour. In fact, sugar is often singled out as public health enemy number one. If you are of a sensitive disposition or you worry about such things, well, then it's best to turn the page.

Ah, good – you're still with me. Now, when brown sugar is baked it takes on the deep flavour of molasses and gives a dark amber glow to this cheesecake. That's all well and good, but you need something sharp to cut into the sweetness. Don't worry; the boozy prunes will do the trick. They need preparing in advance, so make sure you start this dessert the day before you want to eat it.

For twelve:
Vegetable oil, for greasing
300g butter, at room temperature
250g digestive biscuits, broken up
250g soft dark brown sugar
680g soft cream cheese
1 tablespoon treacle
1 teaspoon vanilla extract
125g crème fraîche
75ml double cream
4 medium eggs

For the drunken prunes:
500g prunes
1 Earl Grey teabag
Zest of 1 orange
Zest of 1 lemon
1 cinnamon stick, broken up
100ml brandy

Place the prunes and the teabag in a saucepan, cover with water and bring to the boil. Reduce to a simmer for 10 minutes, then take off the heat and allow to cool. Discard the teabag and drain the prunes. Place the prunes in an airtight plastic container. Add the orange and lemon zest, the cinnamon stick and the brandy. Stir and leave overnight.

Preheat the oven to 180°C/Gas 4. Grease a 25cm loose-bottomed cake tin with a little oil, and line it with baking parchment.

Cut up 100g of the butter into small pieces and mix with the biscuits in a food processor until combined. Put the mixture into the cake tin, pressing as hard as you can with the back of a metal spoon to make

a flat, even base. Bake in the preheated oven for 10 minutes. Remove from the oven and leave to cool. Reduce the oven to 160°C/Gas 3.

Cream the remaining butter and the sugar in a mixer. Add the cream cheese, using a spatula to scrape any mixture down from the sides back into the bowl, so that everything is properly mixed. Next, add the treacle and vanilla, again using the spatula to push down the sides. Add the crème fraîche and cream. Beat the eggs in a separate bowl and then add to the mixture, stirring so that everything is fully incorporated.

Pour the mixture into the cake tin over the biscuit base, transfer to the oven and bake for 20 minutes. Reduce the oven to 150°C/Gas 2 and bake for another 20 minutes. Reduce the oven to 120°C/Gas ½ and cook for yet another 20 minutes. Reduce to 110°C/Gas ¼ and cook for a further 20 minutes. Reduce to 100°C/the very lowest your oven will go, and cook for a final 20 minutes. Open the oven and leave the door ajar until the cheesecake has cooled completely, then refrigerate.

Remove the cheesecake from the fridge 20 minutes before serving. Cut into equal parts, and finish each portion with a generous spoonful of the prunes.

Bourbon Brownies

Brownies vie with apple pie for pole position as the
quintessential American dessert. In Britain we refer to
them, quaintly, as 'chocolate brownies', but in the United
States the word 'chocolate' is implicit, thus redundant.
A brownie should be moist yet firm. Lightness is not to be
encouraged. A proper hit of booze gives our brownie ballast
and gravity, even. You will need to start your preparations
a day in advance.

For eight:
200g dried figs, roughly chopped
150ml bourbon
250g unsalted butter, diced, plus extra for greasing
200g dark cooking chocolate, chopped
100g shelled walnuts, roughly chopped
80g cocoa powder
65g plain flour
1 teaspoon baking powder
200g caster sugar
4 medium eggs

To serve:
Vanilla ice cream

Soak the figs in the bourbon overnight. The next day, strain the figs,
keeping the bourbon for later.

Preheat the oven to 180°C/Gas 4. Grease and line a 20 x 30cm baking
tray with baking parchment.

Melt the butter and chocolate together in a large bowl suspended over
a pan of simmering water. Once melted, remove the bowl from the heat,
and add the figs and walnuts to the chocolate mixture.

In a separate bowl mix the cocoa powder, flour, baking powder and
sugar. Add this to the chocolate mixture and stir well. Beat the eggs
together in a jug, then mix them into the chocolate as well.

Pour the brownie mix into the prepared baking tin and spread out with
the back of a spoon. Bake in the preheated oven for 25 minutes, then
turn the tray around and cook for another 10 minutes or until the tip
of an inserted knife comes out clean.

Remove the baking tray from the oven, prick the brownie all over with
a toothpick, and trickle in the bourbon left over from the soaked figs.
Cut into eight equal portions and serve, while still warm, with a scoop
of vanilla ice cream.

Bourbon, Pecan & Chocolate Cake

Chocolate and booze are very energetic bedfellows – you've already seen them at it in Bourbon Brownies, and this cake is another great excuse to hook them up. Because the pecan nuts are blitzed, this is a flourless dessert and it feels faintly virtuous because of it. Ridiculous, I know. I like to serve the cake warm with a dollop of mascarpone cream.

For twelve:
350g unsalted butter, at room temperature, plus extra for greasing
300g shelled pecans
250g dark chocolate, 70% cocoa content
8 medium eggs, separated
220g caster sugar
100ml bourbon
1 teaspoon vanilla extract

For the mascarpone cream:
450g mascarpone
3 tablespoons icing sugar, sifted
225ml double cream

Preheat the oven to 180°C/Gas 4. Grease and line the base of a 23cm springform cake tin with butter and baking parchment.

Put the pecans on a tray and roast in the preheated oven for 15 minutes. While they are still hot, rub them in a clean tea-towel to remove as much of the skin as possible. Once the pecans have cooled, blend them in a food processor until they resemble breadcrumbs. Reduce the oven to 160°C/Gas 3.

Chop the butter and chocolate into small cubes and place them in a bowl suspended over a pan of boiling water. Leave them to melt, stirring occasionally. Set aside to cool a little.

Meanwhile, in a large bowl, beat the egg yolks and sugar until thick and pale. Slowly add the melted chocolate, 75ml of the bourbon and the vanilla to the egg yolks and sugar. Fold in the pecans. Whisk the egg whites until stiff. Using a large metal spoon scoop one spoonful of the egg white into the chocolate mixture and beat well to loosen, then gently fold in the remaining egg white.

Pour the cake mix into the prepared tin and place on a baking tray. Bake in the preheated oven for 10 minutes. Reduce the heat to 150°C/Gas 2 and cook for a further 1¼–1½ hours. Place a skewer in the middle of the cake – if it comes out clean, remove the cake from the oven and allow it to cool slightly. Poke all over the top of cake with a toothpick and then carefully spoon over the remaining bourbon.

To make the mascarpone cream, whisk together the mascarpone and icing sugar until combined. In a separate bowl whip the cream, then fold through the mascarpone.

Serve the cake in wedges/slices with a large spoonful of mascarpone cream at the side.

Bergamot Marmalade Pudding

Jam-making used to be the preserve (sorry) of the Women's Institute and the legions of enthusiastic amateurs across vast rural swathes of Middle England. But recently it has made inroads into the city. We are fortunate to know a jam-maker in Hackney, East London, who provides us with the most excellent bergamot marmalade. You could use an alternative marmalade of your choosing (or making) if you can't locate a jar of bergamot.

Makes eight:
200g unsalted butter, at room temperature, plus extra for greasing
200g self-raising flour, plus extra for dusting
8 tablespoons bergamot marmalade
200g caster sugar
4 medium eggs, beaten
Fine salt
Finely grated zest of 1 lemon

To serve:
Vanilla ice cream

Preheat the oven to 160°C/Gas 3. Butter really well and flour eight ramekins or small pudding basins – about 125ml each – tapping out any excess flour. Put a tablespoon of the marmalade into each.

In a large bowl, beat the butter and sugar together with a wooden spoon till pale and smooth. Add a quarter of the beaten egg, mixing well. Then add the flour and the remaining egg in alternating batches, always mixing slowly. Then add a pinch of salt and the lemon zest, and mix thoroughly.

Spoon the mixture into the ramekins, about two-thirds full. Then cover each loosely with foil, to allow the mixture to rise during the cooking process. Place the ramekins into a high-sided baking tray. Boil a kettle and pour the hot water into the tray up to about two-thirds of the height of the ramekins and cover the whole tray with foil.

Cook on the middle shelf of the preheated oven for 20 minutes, then turn the tray around and cook for a further 25 minutes. Check one of the puddings with a skewer to make sure the skewer comes out clean.

Turn the puddings out of the ramekins and onto serving plates whilst still warm, sponge-side down, marmalade on top. Add a generous scoop of vanilla ice cream.

Bourbon & Vanilla French Toast

French toast always feels a bit naughty. It must have something to do with the act of frying bread – one of the more transgressive kitchen practices. Eggy bread is a nursery classic, of course, but this version is a childhood staple gone bad. It's as if the kids have run away from home and joined a chapter of the Hell's Angels. With the addition of bourbon, I'd say they're not coming back either.

For eight:
500g dried figs
1 Earl Grey teabag
1 tablespoon vanilla extract
3 tablespoons runny honey
75ml bourbon
6 medium eggs
75ml milk
½ teaspoon ground cinnamon
Fine salt
1 unsliced brioche loaf, shop bought, about 400g
100g unsalted butter
4-6 tablespoons caster sugar

To serve:
Vanilla ice cream

Remove the tops of the figs and cut the figs in half. Place them in a saucepan with the teabag, and just cover with water. Bring to the boil and reduce the heat to low. Remove and discard the teabag. Continue heating to let the liquid reduce by half. Now add 1 teaspoon of the vanilla extract, the honey and 50ml of the bourbon and cook on a low heat for 5–8 minutes so that the liquid becomes syrupy.

Now for the toast. Whisk together the eggs, milk, remaining bourbon, cinnamon, remaining vanilla extract and a pinch of salt. Slice the brioche into a 2.5cm-thick slice for each person.

Place a non-stick frying pan over a medium heat and melt 25g butter in it. Dip two slices of the brioche into the egg mix, making sure the slices are well coated on both sides. Gently lift them out and sprinkle one side with sugar and place that side down into the pan. Sprinkle the top side with sugar. Once the brioche has caramelised to a golden brown colour, about 2 minutes, flip it over to cook the other side. Repeat this with all the remaining brioche slices.

Transfer the brioche slices to the serving plates. Top with figs and place a scoop of vanilla ice cream in the centre.

Dutch Baby

This epic dessert is based on the classic breakfast pancake, sometimes called a Dutch Puff, that came to prominence in the 1940s at Manca's Café in Seattle, Washington. The trademark 'Dutch Baby' was owned by the café until its demise in the 1950s.

At SPUNTINO, the dish has been a bit of a hit. I have known some folk to order one and then, immediately upon finishing, another. It looks like a large Yorkshire pudding, but the combination of batter, ice cream and jam is far nobler, and tastier, than it sounds.

For four:
130g Italian 00 flour
Caster sugar
Fine salt
200ml milk
1 teaspoon vanilla extract
4 medium eggs
Vegetable oil
1 tablespoon melted butter

To serve:
Ice cream
Excellent fruit jam

Preheat the oven to 220°C/Gas 7.

Put the flour, and a very good pinch each of caster sugar and fine salt, into a large bowl and mix. In a separate bowl or jug beat together the milk, vanilla extract and eggs. Make a well in the dry ingredients, pour in the liquid, and mix together until you have a smooth batter.

Use small metal skillets/baking pans of 15cm in diameter, and place them on a baking sheet. Pour about 1 tablespoon of vegetable oil into each pan, then divide the melted butter between them. Put in the oven to heat up.

Once you see the oil is smoking slightly, take the baking tray out of the oven and quickly divide the batter between the four pans. Put straight back into the oven - neither pans nor oven should lose any heat - and bake for about 8-12 minutes until the batter has puffed up like a Yorkshire pudding and is golden in colour.

While they are still warm, sprinkle the puddings generously with caster sugar. Serve with a scoop of vanilla ice cream and a large spoonful of fruit jam.

Pineapple & Liquorice

There are certain flavours that go hand-in-hand: salt and vinegar, strawberries and cream, ham and mustard, pork and apple. You may not expect to see pineapple and liquorice on that list but, take it from me, they are a very cosy couple.

Pineapple and liquorice are like two opposite characters – one fun-loving, the other brooding – who get hitched on a whim and, much to everyone's surprise, end up getting along famously. It's a very successful marriage – a partnership that is greater than the sum of its parts.

The ice cream is best prepared a day in advance.

For eight:
1 ripe pineapple

For the liquorice ice cream:
700ml milk
240ml double cream
200g natural soft liquorice, chopped into small pieces (we used
    6 Panda soft liquorice bars)
16 medium egg yolks
100g soft dark brown sugar
100g caster sugar
4 star anise

Put the milk, cream and liquorice in a pan and heat very gently, stirring, until the liquorice has dissolved, about 20 minutes.

In a mixer, whisk the egg yolks and sugars together until they are thick and pale. Slowly add the hot liquorice mix into the egg mix. Once this is combined, transfer to a clean pan with the star anise and continue stirring with a wooden spoon until the custard thickens - when you draw a finger along the back of the spoon it should leave a line. This will take about 5-8 minutes.

Pass through a fine strainer into a clean bowl, and place the bowl in a tray filled with ice and water. Once the mixture is completely cooled down, churn in an ice-cream machine, following the manufacturer's instructions. Keep in the freezer before serving.

If you don't have a machine you can hand-churn the ice cream. Once the custard mixture has completely cooled pour into a large freezer-proof container. Cover and place in the freezer until starting to become frozen around the edges, about 1-1½ hours. Remove from the freezer

and whisk until smooth using a hand-held electric whisk. Repeat this freezing and whisking process three more times, then leave to freeze completely. The whisking helps prevent ice crystals from forming, resulting in a smooth ice cream.

When ready to serve, remove the top and the outside skin of the pineapple and slice very thinly across to create discs. Lay three or four slices out on each of your plates. Place a scoop of the liquorice ice cream on top of the pineapple and serve immediately.

Bay Ice Cream

We tend to pigeonhole bay in the savoury part of our brain, but it doesn't take a huge leap of imagination to shift it into the sweet. The leaves are deeply perfumed in their fresh state and impart a subtle aromatic flavour once heated and infused into warm milk. I like to serve a couple of scoops of this ice cream with crunchy Pistachio Biscotti (see page 262).

For four:
450ml double cream
150ml milk
6 medium egg yolks
100g caster sugar
12 bay leaves

Pour the cream and milk into a saucepan and bring to the boil. Meanwhile, whisk the egg yolks and sugar until they are pale and thick. Once the milk and cream have come to the boil, slowly add to the eggs and sugar, whisking well as you go.

Put the mixture in a clean pan, add the bay leaves and place over a very low heat. Continue stirring with a wooden spoon until the custard thickens, so that when you draw your finger along the back of the spoon it leaves a line – this will take about 5–8 minutes. Remove from the heat and transfer to a bowl, placing this into another bowl containing iced water, to stop the custard from cooking any more.

Once completely cooled, remove the bay leaves, and pass the custard through a fine strainer. Churn in an ice-cream machine, following the manufacturer's instructions, then transfer to a container and freeze.

If you don't have a machine you can hand-churn the ice cream. Once the custard mixture has completely cooled pour into a large freezer-proof container. Cover and place in the freezer until starting to become frozen around the edges, about 1–1½ hours. Remove from the freezer and whisk until smooth using a hand-held electric whisk. Repeat this freezing and whisking process three more times, then leave to freeze completely. The whisking helps prevent ice crystals from forming, resulting in a smooth ice cream.

Pistachio (or Almond) Biscotti

These little biscuits are so handy for a variety of occasions that I would heartily recommend your making a batch and keeping them in an airtight plastic container. They are the perfect foil for ice cream, adding a pleasant bit of crunch, and also to use as an edible spoon for scooping up the last few mouthfuls. And if, like me, you quite often skip dessert, they are great for dipping into your post-prandial coffee.

For about sixty-four biscuits:
500g plain flour, plus extra for dusting
350g caster sugar
1 teaspoon baking powder
200g pistachio nuts (or almonds), toasted – see page 119
Finely grated zest of 1 lemon
Finely grated zest of 1 orange
Fine salt
5 medium eggs

Preheat the oven to 180°C/Gas 4.

In a large bowl, combine the flour, sugar, baking powder, pistachio nuts (or almonds), lemon and orange zest and a pinch of salt.

Break four of the eggs into a bowl. Separate the remaining egg and add the yolk to the other eggs. Keep the white for later. Mix the eggs and egg yolk together, then pour into the bowl with the flour. Mix this all together very well, then turn out onto a lightly floured surface and knead until your mixture is a pliable dough.

Divide the dough into two, and roll out into two cucumber-shaped logs of around 4–5cm in diameter. Place onto a baking tray lined with baking parchment and than flatten slightly. Brush with the remaining egg white.

Bake in the preheated oven for about 25–30 minutes, until golden. Remove and allow to cool while reducing the oven to 110°C/Gas ¼. Take a very sharp knife and cut the flattened log into thin slices – just under 1cm thick. Lay the biscotti onto baking trays – you may need three or so – each lined with baking parchment. Bake for a further 15–20 minutes, turning over halfway through, until they have firmed up a little. Remove from the oven and leave to cool. The biscotti will harden on cooling.

Store in an airtight plastic container for up to a month.

Pan Pudding

This is a great dessert to make in the New Year with some panettone and panforte, both types of sweet bread that fill the shelves of Italian delis over Christmas. If you are fortunate enough to have them left over from the festivities, even better. They have a miraculous shelf life of several months but tend to be dry even at the best of times, so this is an ingenious way of putting them to good use and creating a lovely variation on a classic bread pudding.

For eight:
50g unsalted butter, plus extra for greasing
4 medium eggs, beaten
400ml milk
50ml whipping cream
125g caster sugar
450–500g leftover panettone
100g leftover panforte
Icing sugar, for dusting

For the crème anglaise:
6 medium egg yolks
125g caster sugar
500ml milk
1 vanilla pod, split

Preheat the oven to 180°C/Gas 4. Butter eight ramekins - about 125ml each - and set aside.

For the puddings, put the beaten eggs, milk, cream and sugar into a mixing bowl and whisk well to combine. Cut the panettone and the panforte into rough slices that will fit into the ramekins. Liberally douse the slices in the egg and milk mixture and layer them alternately in the ramekins.

Melt the 50g butter in a saucepan over a gentle heat and brush the tops of the puddings with it. Place the ramekins in a baking tray. Boil a kettle and pour the hot water into the tray up to about two-thirds of the height of the ramekins. Bake in the preheated oven for 45 minutes. When done, they should be nicely browned but not dry.

While the puddings are cooking, make the crème anglaise. Put the egg yolks in a bowl, then whisk in the sugar until thick and pale. Bring the milk to the boil with the vanilla pod. Remove from the heat and allow to cool slightly. (Remove the vanilla pod, and save for another recipe.) Slowly add the warmed milk to the egg and sugar mix while beating

with a wooden spoon. Pour the mixture into a clean saucepan and set over a low to medium heat. Continue to beat the mixture whilst heating, until it resembles custard and you are able to draw a line with your finger on the back of the spoon. This will take about 5-8 minutes. Pass through a fine sieve into a jug, then cover the surface directly with clingfilm to prevent a skin forming.

Sift the icing sugar over the tops of the puddings and serve them immediately with the warm crème anglaise - you may need to reheat it if it has become too cold.

Blood Orange & Campari Jelly

I have nostalgic memories of jelly from childhood birthday parties. Back then, the jellies were always made in novelty moulds and had a thin, watery consistency that was perfect for sucking through the gaps between your new front teeth. They were improbably coloured – shocking pink, thermonuclear orange or Kryptonite green – and invariably accompanied by cheap, sugary ice cream.

How times (and tastes) have changed. This jelly is a celebration of the bitter rather than the sweet, and would be far more appropriate at a fortieth birthday party than a fourth.

For four:
4 gelatine leaves
150g caster sugar
395ml freshly squeezed blood orange juice
1 tablespoon Campari
100ml double cream, lightly whipped
Biscotti, to serve - see page 262

Soak the gelatine in a bowl of cold water for a few minutes.

Tip the sugar into a pan and pour in 150ml water. Set over a low heat until the sugar has dissolved, then turn up the heat and simmer for a few minutes. Mix 50ml of this syrup with the orange juice and Campari in another pan.

Gently warm 75ml only of this juice mixture in yet another pan then turn off the heat. Remove the gelatine from the cold water, squeeze out any excess liquid and add to the warmed juice mixture, stirring until completely dissolved. Add this to the rest of the juice mixture, stir well and pass through a fine strainer into a jug.

Pour the liquid jelly into four small pudding moulds - about 150ml. You could pour the jelly into four small glasses, in which case you could reduce the number of gelatine leaves to three. Place on a tray lined with a cloth and chill for 3 hours or until set.

Once set, turn the jellies out of the moulds onto serving plates or serve in their glasses, with the cream on the side. Serve with biscotti.

Pistachio Cheesecake

The pistachio is the prince of nuts. It leaves almonds, hazels, pecans and walnuts in the shade. Pistachios are delicious raw or lightly roasted and, as an ingredient, they add an exotic tang and a very distinctive green glow.

You'll need to do a bit of detective work to get hold of pistachio paste and morello cherry purée. They are readily available in swanky department-store food halls, but haven't made it to high-street supermarket shelves just yet. You can find them from online suppliers, however, so my advice is to plan ahead.

For sixteen:
150g butter, diced into small cubes, plus extra for greasing
300g digestive biscuits (20 biscuits)
200g pistachio nuts
550g caster sugar
700g cream cheese
4 large egg yolks
200g crème fraîche
3 tablespoons cornflour
100g pistachio paste
300g morello cherry purée

Preheat the oven to 180°C/Gas 4. Grease and line the base and sides of a 23cm springform cake tin with baking parchment.

Put the digestive biscuits into a large mixing bowl and, using the end of a solid wooden rolling pin, crush to crumbs. Melt the butter and stir into the biscuit crumbs until thoroughly combined. Press the mix as hard and as flat as you can into the prepared cake tin. Bake in the preheated oven for 10 minutes. Remove and leave to cool.

Meanwhile, roast the pistachio nuts on a baking sheet for 10 minutes then leave to cool on the tray. Turn the oven down to 120°C/Gas ½.

Put 350g of the caster sugar in a saucepan with 4 tablespoons of water over a gentle heat. The sugar will turn to caramel without the need for stirring or shaking. (Please resist the strong temptation to shake the pan, as this might cause crystallisation.) When the sugar has turned to a thick, golden liquid, pour it evenly over the roasted pistachios and set aside to solidify.

Now put the cream cheese, remaining sugar, egg yolks, crème fraîche, cornflour and pistachio paste into a very large mixing bowl. Using a whisk or a wooden spoon, or a combination of both, thoroughly mix the ingredients together. Pour the mix over the biscuit base, and smooth the surface. Place on a baking tray and carefully transfer to the oven. Bake for 1½ hours - the filling should still wobble in the centre.

Turn the oven off but do not remove the cheesecake - leave it in the cooling oven for a further hour. This will stop the centre from collapsing. Remove from the oven, and allow to cool completely. Release from the parchment paper with a palette knife warmed under a hot tap, and chill until ready to serve.

When you are ready to serve, heat the cherry purée gently in a saucepan, adjusting with a little added sugar if necessary. Break the pistachio caramel brittle into small pieces by covering the sheet with a tea-towel and smashing with a rolling pin. Slice the cheesecake carefully with a warmed palette knife, place on plates, and finish with a generous drizzle of the cherry coulis and a scattering of pistachio brittle.

Peanut Butter
& Jelly Sandwich

The PBJ (as it is affectionately known) is one of the dishes
that defines SPUNTINO. It is playful, sure, but it has serious
intentions. It takes its inspiration from that blue-collar classic
of white bread, peanut butter and jam – a perfect and
nutritional balance of fruit, nut and grain. Ahem.

Although our version shares a name with the lunchbox
staple, don't be fooled: it's two blocks of peanut butter ice
cream shaped to look like sliced white and filled with coulis
to represent raspberry jam.

Prepare the ice cream a day in advance – it will taste
better and you will be able to slice it more easily.

For eight:
180g caster sugar
8 medium egg yolks
450g peanut butter
1 teaspoon vanilla extract
Fine salt
250ml whole milk
500ml whipping cream
Butter, for greasing

For the peanut brittle:
175g salted peanuts
Vegetable oil, for greasing
175g caster sugar

For the raspberry coulis:
125g raspberries
60g caster sugar

To start the ice cream, place the sugar and egg yolks into a mixer and
whisk until pale and thick.

Melt the peanut butter by placing it in a bowl suspended over a pan
of boiling water. Add the vanilla extract and a pinch of salt.

Place the milk and cream in another saucepan and bring to the boil,
then remove from the heat.

While the mixer is still running, add the melted peanut butter and the
cream mix to the sugar and egg yolks. Do this slowly so that the hot
mix doesn't cook the eggs. Once fully incorporated, pass through a fine
strainer into a clean saucepan.

Place on the stove at the lowest temperature and, with a wooden spoon, keep stirring the mixture until the custard has thickened and you can draw a line across the back of the spoon with your finger. This will take about 5–8 minutes. Transfer to a clean bowl, and place this into a tray of iced water. Once it has cooled down, churn the mixture in an ice-cream machine following the manufacturer's instructions.

If you don't have an ice-cream machine you can hand-churn the ice cream. Once the custard mixture has completely cooled pour into a large freezer-proof container. Cover and place in the freezer until starting to become frozen around the edges, about 1–1½ hours. Remove from the freezer and whisk until smooth using a hand-held electric whisk. Repeat this freezing and whisking process three more times.

continued overleaf

While the ice cream is churning, prepare your ice-cream tin. Rub the inside of a 900g loaf tin with butter and line with a strip of baking parchment. Place in the freezer until the ice cream has finished churning. Once churned, whether by machine or hand, put the ice-cream mixture into the tin and freeze.

The next day, take a steel palette knife and run it under hot water, then run along the sides of the tin to help release the ice cream. Turn it out onto a chopping board and divide into eight slices using a sharp knife, regularly running the knife under hot water so that it cuts smoothly. Once you have cut the slices, cut them diagonally to create triangles. Put them on a tray with layers of baking paper on both sides, wrap well and return to the freezer until you are ready to serve.

Now for the peanut brittle. Preheat the oven to 180°C/Gas 4. Place the peanuts on a baking sheet in a single layer and roast in the oven for 10–12 minutes, until golden brown. Set aside to cool, then tip into a bowl. Grease the tray with a little oil. Put the sugar in a saucepan and place it over a medium to high heat. Let the sugar dissolve a little, then start whisking to keep it moving and so that the outer edges don't burn and ruin the caramel. Once the syrup has become a rich caramel colour and there are no lumps, pour over the roasted peanuts in the bowl, and stir well. Tip out onto the greased baking sheet, making sure it is evenly spread. Leave to cool.

Once the peanut brittle has cooled completely and is hard, break the sheet into pieces and put them into a food processor. Blitz until you have small chunks.

Finally, for the coulis, put half the raspberries in a saucepan with 60ml water and the sugar over a high heat. Bring to the boil, then reduce the heat to medium. Reduce the liquid by half, then add the remaining raspberries and bring back to the boil. Remove from the heat immediately and transfer to a clean container.

Once the raspberry coulis has cooled down, you are ready to assemble the dish. First scatter half the peanut brittle equally on each of your plates, then place a triangle of the peanut butter ice cream on top. Now spoon over some raspberry coulis so that it covers the ice cream triangle completely, then place another triangle on top. Finally, scatter the remaining peanut brittle equally over the top of the ice cream. Serve immediately.

Williamsburg

Drinks

SPUNTINO is a bar with an identity crisis. When I designed
it, there was never any doubt in my mind that it would feature
a horseshoe-shaped counter, with stools on three sides. This
would allow the servers to remain at the centre of the action,
always (whether they liked it or not) putting on a show, while
every diner got a ring-side seat.

A consequence of being sat at this bar (you are only
human after all) is that you want a drink. Allow me, then,
to introduce some of SPUNTINO's bartenders – Becky, Ben,
Benny, Eloise, Josie, Raf and Tom – who will serve up their
favourites in the pages that follow.

I should warn you, if you are of a linguistically delicate
disposition, that we have a weakness for puns when it comes
to the naming of our concoctions. I am so very sorry. You will
find recipes here for the Dill Murray and the Ted Damson.
We also have a very successful Rhubarbra Streisand. I confess
that I delight in making a bartender cringe with a choice
cocktail name pun. My favourite suggestion was for a trio of
cocktails called the Brat Pack. It would consist of the Frank
Ginatra, the Dean Martini and the Sammy Davis Juniper.
Oh how we groaned. Others that got away: the Tequila
Mockingbird, the Quincey Jones, and a cocktail made with
pickle juice and a famous Tennessee sour-mash whiskey
called the Jack Pickleson.

I'm not especially fussy about tableware, but a well-
chosen cocktail glass will always flatter a carefully made
beverage. We have myriad pretty and unusual glasses in our
arsenal – tumblers, highballs, schooners, coupes, cups and
tankards – the result of many happy hours browsing flea
markets and junk shops. We like to serve our cocktails in
mismatched glassware – diners often remark on this habit
approvingly – which is a trick I have adopted at home too.
It is also rather impressive to serve your drinks in glasses that
have been chilling in the freezer for half an hour. The frosting
on the outside of the glass gives a real sense of attention to
detail; the drinks will stay cold longer, too.

To finish with, a note on terminology. A rocks glass is
a short, solid tumbler. A highball glass is tall and straight.
A cocktail glass is a pretty, conical vessel with a stem. A twist
is simply a long strip of lemon or orange skin, which is twisted
over a drink to release the oil and then dropped into it. And
finally, sugar syrup is caster sugar dissolved in an equal
volume of water.

Homebrews

Although the word 'homebrew' conjures up images of illegal distilling equipment, dodgy barrels of hooch and contraband moonshine, it's actually much tamer than that. A homebrew is simply a bottle of off-the-shelf booze flavoured with something else. It's amazing what you can do with a flask of spirit and a few well-chosen herbs, spices, fruits and vegetables.

These homebrews are just three of the dozens we make at SPUNTINO. They are all used in the cocktails you will find in these pages.

Earl Grey Gin

To make 1 x 70cl bottle:
Put 6 heaped teaspoons mild Earl Grey tea leaves into a bottle of gin. Seal and let rest for 2 hours. Don't leave it any longer or it'll be too bitter. Pour the gin through a coffee filter in a funnel into a separate cleaned and dried bottle.

Use in an Earl Grey Martini (see page 288).

Apple Pie Bourbon

To make 1 x 70cl bottle:
Core and slice three red dessert apples, and place in a Kilner jar with a cracked cinnamon stick and a split vanilla pod. Pour over a bottle of good bourbon. Seal and leave for 40 days. Once a week, turn the jar over a few times. On the 40th day, strain into a fresh bottle using a sieve and a funnel.

The bourbon-soaked apples should be used as a garnish in an Apple Pie Old Fashioned (see page 295).

Dill Gin

To make 1 x 70cl bottle:
Take a full bottle of gin and empty about 100ml into a clean glass. Set aside. Push a fresh bunch of dill into the bottle. If there is any room for more gin, top it up with the excess in the glass. Seal and leave for three days. Straining is optional.

Use in a Dill Murray (see page 293).

Old Fashioned

'Late nights in Soho mean three things to me – loud music, neon lights and cherry-red Old Fashioneds. The best nights at SPUNTINO are the ones that leave you bourbon-stained. One evening I made two gents a succession of Old Fashioneds. I lost count of how many. By the end of the night, when we had to turn off the Springsteen that had been blaring for hours, they belted out 'Born to Run' a cappella-style in its entirety, resulting in a standing ovation from the whole restaurant. Some things can only be achieved by way of bourbon.'
  —*Eloise*

For one:
Rocks glass

2 Amarena cherries
4 dashes of Angostura bitters
2 dashes of orange bitters
1 dash of sugar syrup
2 orange twists
Ice
50ml bourbon
1 teaspoon juice from the cherry jar

You need to take your time with this drink. It is important to let the ingredients get to know each other slowly. Put one of the cherries, the bitters, the sugar syrup and one of the twists in a rocks glass and muddle - bar speak for mashing up with the back of a spoon. Half fill the glass with ice and add half the bourbon. Stir. Continue to build with ice and stir until all the bourbon is used. Garnish with the other orange twist, another cherry and the juice from the cherry jar.

The Ted Damson

'Everyone has a favourite *Cheers* character, be it Norm, Woody or whoever. For our bartender Larry Webster, who created this drink, it was Sam.

Diane: And everyone knows that hate is not the opposite of love. Indifference is.

Sam: Well, whatever you say. I really don't care.'
—*Tom*

For one:
Cocktail glass, chilled

40ml vodka
1 tablespoon damson vodka (Sipsmith make a good one)
2 teaspoons lemon juice
2 teaspoons sugar syrup
4 dashes of Fee Brothers rhubarb bitters
Ice
Lemon twist

Fill a jug with all the liquid ingredients and a good handful of ice and stir vigorously for 20 seconds with a long-handled spoon. Strain into a chilled cocktail glass and garnish with the lemon twist.

Cynar Gin Fizz

'A variation on a gin fizz that uses Campari's obscure cousin, Cynar. With a base of artichoke – not quite as bonkers as it sounds – this Italian apéritif is the backbone of the drink. In fact, you might like to up the quantities and make a jug for a sunny afternoon. It's like Pimm's with attitude.'
  —*Raf*

For one:
Highball glass

25ml gin
25ml Cynar
2 teaspoons lemon juice
2 teaspoons sugar syrup
Ice
Prosecco, for topping up
2 slices of cucumber

Put the gin, Cynar, lemon juice and sugar syrup into a jug with a large handful of ice and stir vigorously for 20 seconds with a long-handled spoon. Fill a highball glass with fresh ice and strain the mix onto it. Top up with Prosecco and garnish with cucumber.

Gin Palace Shandy

'The Gin Palace Shandy is a play on a classic shandy, bringing together gin and ale, perhaps the two most iconic drinks London has seen. By swapping traditional lemonade for a punchy base of gin and lemon juice, we fortify the pale ale rather than dumbing it down.'
  —*Raf*

For one:
300ml glass mug, chilled

35ml gin
25ml lemon juice
25ml sugar syrup
Ice
Can or bottle of pale ale, chilled
Lemon twist

Put the gin, lemon juice and sugar syrup into a jug with a large handful of ice and stir vigorously for 20 seconds with a long-handled spoon. Strain into a beer mug that has been left in the freezer for 30 minutes and top up with chilled pale ale. Garnish with a lemon twist.

Earl Grey Martini

'In beverage terms, what could possibly be more English than
gin? Well, Earl Grey tea, I suppose. This cocktail effectively
mixes both in the same glass and is a refreshing variation on
a classic drink. But be careful – they are very moreish. It might
be wise to remember the words of Dorothy Parker:
  I like to have a martini,
  Two at the very most.
  After three I'm under the table,
  After four I'm under my host.'
  —*Ben*

For one:
Cocktail glass, chilled

Ice
3 dashes of orange bitters
50ml Earl Grey Gin - see page 281
2 teaspoons sugar syrup
Orange twist

Fill a jug with ice. Add the bitters, stir to coat the ice with them, and
strain away any melted water. Add the gin and sugar syrup and stir
again for 20 seconds. Strain into a chilled cocktail glass and garnish
with an orange twist.

Perfect Manhattan

'Sometimes all you want is a classic – no bells, no whistles,
definitely no umbrellas – just a straight-up drink that tastes
like what it is. The Manhattan, like the best drinks, has
various tales of origin but one thing is for sure – it was first
made around 1860. I like the way that such a simple drink can
vary so much but remain distinctive. A Perfect Manhattan is
my liquid dessert of choice and the kind of drink you order in
a dark bar, late at night, just before heading out into the cold.'
 —*Josie*

For one:
Cocktail glass, chilled

Ice
40ml rye whiskey
1 tablespoon sweet vermouth
1 tablespoon dry vermouth
1 Amarena cherry

Fill a glass jug with ice and add the rye and the vermouths. Stir for
20 seconds and strain into a chilled cocktail glass. Garnish with a cherry.

Seelbach

'This clean, refreshing cocktail is a staff favourite – always
a good sign. Despite being quite complex – floral, herbal
and spicy from the bitters – it slips down easily, with a dry
finish from the triple sec and Prosecco. It's a bourbon cocktail
that even those who don't like bourbon get on with, and an
excellent apéritif, though I'd never turn one down at the end
of a meal either.'
　　—Josie

For one:
Rocks glass

5 dashes Angostura bitters
5 dashes Peychaud's bitters
25ml bourbon
1 tablespoon triple sec
Ice
Prosecco, for topping up
Lemon twist

Add the bitters, bourbon and triple sec to a jug filled with ice. Stir
with a long-handled spoon for 20 seconds and then strain into a rocks
glass filled with clean ice. Top up with Prosecco and garnish with
a lemon twist.

Sazerac

'The Sazerac is my favourite cocktail from the SPUNTINO menu and my poison of choice after a busy night. It's an ancient drink hailing from New Orleans, named after the brand of cognac originally used to make it. I especially love the way we serve it in a vintage silver-plated teacup. Any customer who orders a Sazerac has my immediate respect.'
—*Benny*

For one:
Beautiful vintage glass or silver-plated teacup

2 teaspoons absinthe
Ice
50ml rye whiskey
4 dashes of Peychaud's bitters
1 teaspoon sugar syrup
Lemon twist

Coat the inside of the glass or teacup with the absinthe and fill it with ice. Set aside in the freezer to chill for 5 minutes. Fill a jug with ice, add the rye, bitters and sugar syrup and stir gently for 20 seconds. Retrieve the glass/teacup, discard the absinthe and ice and strain in the mixture from the jug. Garnish with a lemon twist.

The Dill Murray

'Recently I went to the races with the idea of backing horses that were definitely going to win. This sensible plan fell by the wayside when I saw a horse called Cocktails at Dawn. It was 50 to 1, and I lost thirty quid. I don't advise choosing your horses based on ridiculous names, but I always recommend it with drinks. Past SPUNTINO favourites have included the Cardamom Electra and a version of an eggnog called Noggin' on Heaven's Door. Try the Dill Murray – odds on you'll be backing a winner.'

—*Becky*

For one:
Cocktail glass, chilled

35ml Dill Gin - see page 281
2 teaspoons elderflower cordial
2 teaspoons lemon juice
2 teaspoons sugar syrup
2 teaspoons egg white
Ice
Sprig of dill

Put all the liquid ingredients, including the egg white, into a cocktail shaker and shake vigorously for 5 seconds without using ice. This is called a dry shake and it is important to incorporate the egg white. Now add a large handful of ice and shake again, this time for 15 seconds. Strain into the chilled cocktail glass and garnish with the sprig of dill.

Apple Pie Old Fashioned

'Every now and again we make a batch of a homebrew we call
Apple Pie Bourbon. You will find the recipe on page 281.
It takes forty days to fully mature and the day we open it is a
bit of an event. Apple Pie Bourbon Day is a regular celebration
throughout the winter at SPUNTINO and die-hard punters
will mark the date on their calendar. It is the principal
ingredient in our Apple Pie Old Fashioned, a warm and spicy
variation on a classic. The bottle never lasts more than a single
service; fourteen large shots and when it's gone, it's gone.'
—*Eloise*

For one:
Rocks glass

Ice
2 dashes of Angostura bitters
2 dashes of Fee Brothers Whiskey Barrel Aged Bitters
1 teaspoon sugar syrup
50ml Apple Pie Bourbon – see page 281 – plus a piece of
    the bourbon-soaked apple

Half fill the rocks glass with ice and add the bitters and the sugar syrup.
Stir. Now add half the bourbon and stir again. Add more ice, stirring all
the while, and continue to build with ice, slowly adding the bourbon
and stirring until all the bourbon is used. Garnish with a slice of the
booze-soaked apple from the homebrew.

Oven Temperatures

The temperatures in these recipes are for conventional ovens. Fan-assisted oven temperatures should be lowered by 10°C or even 20°C (1 or 2 Gas marks) depending on your oven.

Sourcing Ingredients in the US

Double cream and caster sugar, key ingredients for some of the recipes in this book, may be difficult to come by in American stores. You can use heavy or whipping cream and superfine sugar in their place. Also note that self-raising flour, in the recipe on page 253, can be made at home by adding one teaspoon of baking powder to 110g (4oz) plain flour.

Conversions for Dry Measures

Metric	Imperial	Metric	Imperial
10g	½oz	175g	6oz
20g	¾oz	200g	7oz
25g	1oz	225g	8oz
40g	1½oz	250g	9oz
50g	2oz	275g	10oz
60g	2½oz	350g	12oz
75g	3oz	450g	1lb
110g	4oz	700g	1lb 8oz
125g	4½oz	900g	2lb
150g	5oz	1.35kg	3lb

Conversions for Liquid Measures

15ml	1 tbsp	½ fl oz
30ml	⅛ cup	1 fl oz
60ml	¼ cup	2 fl oz
120ml	½ cup	4 fl oz
240ml	1 cup	8 fl oz
480ml	1 pint	16 fl oz

Acknowledgements

I am indebted to Rachel O'Sullivan, SPUNTINO's founding head chef, for the restaurant's principal recipes and for her invaluable enthusiasm and palate. Thanks also go to Marton Keve for additional recipes, and for preparing all the dishes for photography.

I am grateful to Jenny Zarins for surpassing all expectations with such beautiful photography, and thanks to Tabitha Hawkins for help with stage-managing the shoots.

I salute David Tanguy and David Bate at Praline Design and I genuflect to my brilliant editors at Bloomsbury, Richard Atkinson and Natalie Bellos, assisted splendidly by Alison Glossop. Thanks also to copyeditor Susan Fleming and home economist Emily Kydd for their excellent work on the recipes, and to production manager Marina Asenjo.

A big thank you to Cathryn Summerhayes and Siobhan O'Neill at William Morris Endeavour, Dominique Fraser at Fraser Communications and Sophie Laurimore at Factual Management.

I have had such great support from everyone at SPUNTINO HQ, but in particular Luke Bishop, Benny Locke and Jason Wass. Thanks to Alice Edwards, Izzy England, Arno Karsten, Tom Ross and Charlotte Whiting, too. I'd also like to mention prominent ex-SPUNTINIANS Ajax Kentish, Sean Blake and Eloise Ohlson de Fine.

In New York, my thanks and love go to April Bloomfield, Ken Friedman, Keith McNally and Danny Meyer, all titans in their field. There was also significant support from Richard Bacon, Simon Ford, Graham Paling and Sasha Petraske. Thanks guys.

Penultimately, all hail Richard Beatty, my best friend and business partner, for his constant support and encouragement.

And finally, much love and gratitude to my wife Jules McNally Norman for helping me keep perspective and for regular reassurance, proof reading, brow-mopping and tea.

This book is dedicated to Jules and to my children Oliver, Martha and Mabel.

Bloomsbury Publishing
An imprint of Bloomsbury Publishing Plc

50 Bedford Square, London WC1B 3DP, UK
1385 Broadway, NY 10018, USA

www.bloomsbury.com

BLOOMSBURY and the Diana logo are trademarks of Bloomsbury Publishing Plc

First published in 2015

British Library Cataloguing-in-Publication Data
A catalogue record for this book is available from the British Library.

Library of Congress Cataloguing-in-Publication data has been applied for.

ISBN: 978-1-4088-4717-6

2 4 6 8 10 9 7 5 3 1

Copyeditor: Susan Fleming
Design: Praline
Photographer: Jenny Zarins
Prop stylist: Tabitha Hawkins
Indexer: Hilary Bird

Printed and bound in China by C&C Offset Printing Co Ltd

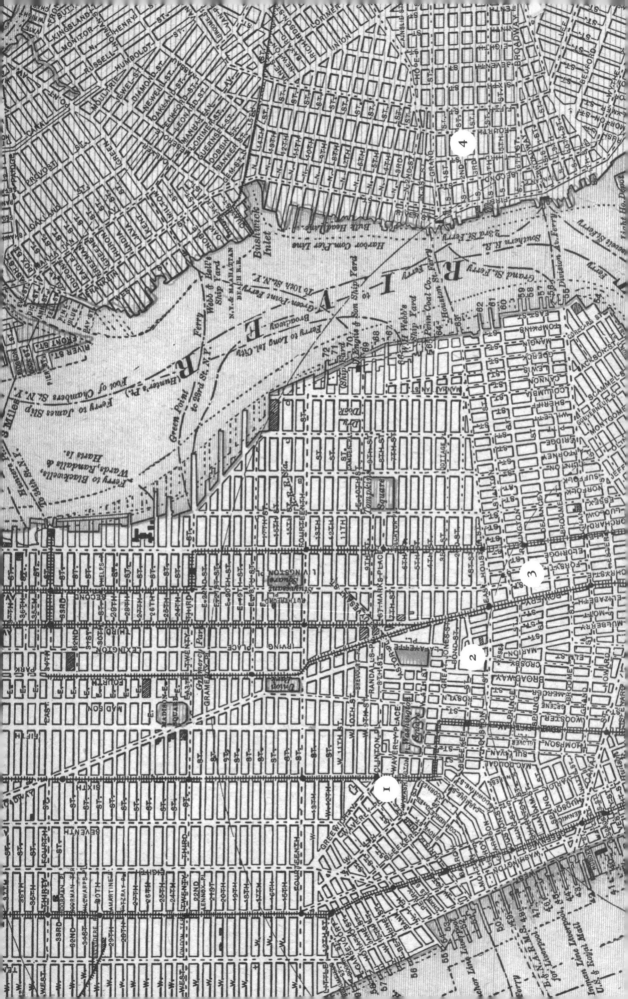